THE LANGUAGE
DREAMS

THE LANGUAGE OF
DREAMS

DAVID FONTANA

WITH PAINTINGS BY PETER MALONE

DUNCAN BAIRD PUBLISHERS

LONDON

The Language of Dreams
David Fontana

This edition first published in the United Kingdom and Ireland in
2003 by Duncan Baird Publishers Ltd
Sixth Floor, Castle House
75–76 Wells Street
London W1T 3QH

Conceived, created and designed by Duncan Baird Publishers Ltd.

First published in Great Britain in 1994 by Pavilion Books Limited
26 Upper Ground, London SE1 9PD

Editor: Joanne Clay
Designer: Gail Jones
Managing Editor: Christopher Westhorp
Managing Designer: Manisha Patel
Commissioned Artwork: Peter Malone
Commissioned Photography and Photographic Illustrations:
   Jules Selmes
Picture Research: Jan Croot
Props: Eliza Solesbury

British Library Cataloguing-in-Publication Data:
A catalogue record for this book is available from the British
Library

ISBN: 1-904292-62-3

10 9 8 7 6 5 4 3 2 1

Main text typeset in Garamond
Colour reproduction by Colourscan, Singapore
Printed and bound in Singapore by Imago

CONTENTS

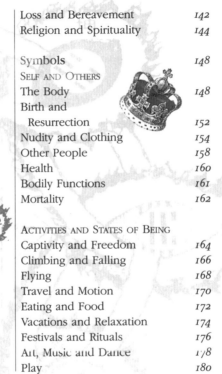

Contents

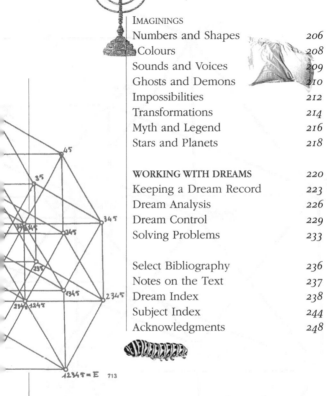

Contents

PERSPECTIVES ON THE DREAM WORLD

We live in two worlds, the waking world with its laws of science, logic and social behaviour, and the elusive, mysterious world of dreaming. In the dream world, fantastic happenings, images and transformations are normal currency. Such dream experiences are often suffused with a depth of emotion or visionary insight that can surpass waking experience.

Historically, most of the world's cultures have believed that dreams come from an outside source and are visitations from the gods. Until relatively recently, the horrifying apparitions that emerge in nightmares were interpreted as demons intent on seducing the innocent. Such obsolete interpretations are explored in the first half of this chapter.

Modern dream study begins with Sigmund Freud (1856–1939), who located dreams in the unconscious, where our repressed instincts and desires dwell. The ground-breaking theories of Carl Jung (1875–1961) concerning archetypes and the collective unconscious were in many ways a direct response to Freud. Inevitably, these two figures loom large in a book on dreaming.

The identification of REM (Rapid Eye Movement) sleep in 1953 brought technology to bear on dream research, in order to explore the physiology of dreaming and the relationship between dreams and sleep. The latter half of "Perspectives on the Dream World" analyzes this relationship, and concludes by demonstrating how dream precognition, once seen as the domain of mystics and charlatans, has in recent years been studied and tested in dream laboratories.

DREAMING THROUGH HISTORY

Throughout history we have sought to fathom the meanings of our dreams, searching them for insights into our present lives and for predictions of our future. The most ancient civilizations believed that dreams carried messages from the gods. Cuneiform tablets from Assyria and Babylon dating from the end of the fourth millennium BCE, depict a society whose priests and kings received warnings in their dreams from the deity Zaqar. The Gilgamesh epic, the great tale of a Mesopotamian hero-king written in the Akkadian language during the first millennium BCE, is full of dream accounts, many replete with divine omens of danger or victory.

Ancient Jewish tradition anticipated modern dream theory by recognizing that the life-circumstances of the dreamer are as important in interpretation as the dream content. In the sixth century BCE the Israelite prophet Daniel correctly interpreted one of the Babylonian king Nebuchadnezzar's dreams as predicting the monarch's imminent seven years of madness (Daniel 4: 535). Another Israelite, Joseph, who was sold into slavery in Egypt, rose to a position of power by correctly interpreting Pharaoh's dream foretelling seven plentiful and seven lean years in the ancient kingdom (Genesis 41: 138).

The ancient Greeks built more than 300 shrines to

Dreaming Through History

serve as dream oracles. Mortals in these shrines were subjected to the soporific power of Hypnos, god of sleep. Once they had passed into slumber, the god Morpheus could communicate with his adepts, passing warnings and prophecies to them in their dreams. Many of these shrines became famous as centres of healing. The sick would sleep there, hoping for a visitation from Aesculapius, the god of healing. While the dreamer was sleeping, surrounded by harmless yellow snakes, he would provide remedies for their physical ills, sometimes effecting immediate cures.

Plato, writing in the fourth century BCE, believed the liver to be the seat of dreams. He attributed some dreams to the gods, but others to what in the *Republic* he called the "lawless wild beast nature which peers out in sleep". While Plato thus anticipated Freud by more than 2,000 years, his pupil Aristotle foreshadowed twentieth-century scientific rationalism by arguing that dreams were triggered by purely sensory causes. Despite such cautionary voices, popular belief in the divinatory power of dreams remained widespread.

In the second century CE, the Sophist philosopher Artemidorus of Daldis drew together the wisdom of earlier centuries in five highly influential dream books, the *Oneirocritica* (from the Greek *oneiros*, "a dream"). Artemidorus identified the importance of the dreamer's personality in dream analysis, and observed the nature and frequency of sexual symbols.

Oriental dream traditions are more philosophical and contemplative than Western ones, and lay more emphasis upon the dreamer's state of mind than upon the predictive power of the dream itself. Chinese sages recognized that consciousness has different levels, and when interpreting dreams they took account of the physical condition and horoscope of the dreamer as well as of

Dreaming Through History

the time of year. They believed that consciousness leaves the body during sleep and travels in otherworldly realms: to arouse the dreamer abruptly, before mind and body are reunited, could be highly dangerous.

Indian *rsis*, or seers, also believed in the multi-layered nature of consciousness, recognizing the discrete states of waking, dreaming, dreamless sleep and *samadhi*, the bliss that follows enlightenment. Hindu tradition also emphasizes the importance of individual dream images, relating them to a wider system incorporating the symbolic attributes of gods and demons. The Hindu belief that some symbols are universal while others are personal to the dreamer, foreshadows the work of both Freud and Jung.

In the West, little progress was made in the study of dreams in the centuries after Artemidorus. The Arabs, however, influenced by Eastern wisdom, produced dream dictionaries and a wealth of interpretations. Muhammad rose from obscurity to found Islam following a dream in which he received his prophetic call – thereafter dreams came to the forefront of religious orthodoxy.

The belief that dreams could be divinely inspired persisted during early Christendom, and in the fourth century CE was part of the teaching of Church fathers such as saints John Chrysostom, Augustine and Jerome. However, by the end of the Middle Ages, the Church had discounted the possibility that such dream messages could be relayed to the average believer, saying God's revelation was only in and through the Church itself.

However, dream interpretation was too strongly rooted in popular consciousness to be readily dismissed. With the increasing availability of printed books in Europe from the fifteenth century onward, dream dictionaries proliferated, mostly based on the works of Artemidorus. And even though the scientific rationalists of the eighteenth century believed that dream interpretation was a

Dreaming Through History

form of primitive superstition, popular interest in dreams gathered strength. Moreover, dreams began to feature as prominent themes in literature and art, as the new Romanticism, led by visionaries such as William Blake and Goethe, placed emphasis on the importance of the individual and the creative power of the imagination.

Later, European philosophers such as Johann Gottlieb Fichte (1762–1814) and Johann Friedrich Herbart (1776–1841) began to regard dreams as worthy of serious psychological study, paving the way for the revolution in dream theory that began in the late nineteenth century with Sigmund Freud (1856–1939).

In 1899 Freud published his monumental work *The Interpretation of Dreams* (see pages 48–55). His neurological studies had convinced him of the role that dreams could play in providing access to the unconscious, or *id*. For Freud, this was primarily the seat of desires and impulses, usually of a sexual nature, that are often repressed by the conscious mind. Most dreams, he believed, are simple wish-fulfilments, or expressions of repressed ideas that force their way into our consciousness when our egos relax control during sleep. Freud developed techniques in psychoanalysis to interpret the coded symbolism of dream images, which he claimed could serve as a key to the unconscious mind.

The views of the Swiss-born psychologist Carl Jung (1875–1961) on dreams form an important counterpoint to those of Freud. According to Jung's theory of the "collective unconscious" (see page 57), the mind contains a vast internal reservoir of symbolism that we draw upon in our dreams. Stored in the collective unconscious are the "archetypes" (see pages 65–77), the profoundly resonating images and themes that not only inform the world's myths and religious and symbolic systems, but also populating our most universally meaningful dreams.

Dreaming Through History

Dreaming Through History

Although many new techniques of dream interpretation have sprung up in recent times, psychoanalysis and Jungian analysis continue to be at the core of psychological investigation into dreams and their symbolic meaning.

The greatest breakthrough in dream research in the second half of the twentieth century was the discovery in 1953 of REM (Rapid Eye Movement) sleep, when the most vivid dreams occur (see opposite). When sleepers are awakened during REM periods, dream recall is greatly enhanced, enabling more accurate analysis of the images, symbols and other psychic events that punctuate our sleep.

However, much work remains to be done before a fully fledged science of dreaming is constructed. In the meantime, through dream workshops and other forms of analysis, we are building up a corpus of case studies that will, it is hoped, form an invaluable body of evidence for the dream scientists of the future.

DREAMS AND SLEEP

We now know that probably everybody dreams. Although many of us forget most or all of the dreams that have visited us during the night, normally we dream for about one fifth of the time that we are asleep. Most of our "big" dreams come to us during REM (Rapid Eye Movement) sleep, and are filled with narratives, symbols and detailed dream scenery. As we fall asleep and in the moments before waking, we experience the fleeting images of *hypnogogic* and *hypnopompic* dreams (see page 27). We dream at other phases of the night as well, and although some of these dreams are indistinguishable from REM dreams, most are fragmentary, less meaningful, less vivid, and rarely remembered upon waking.

In addition to REM, there are four other distinct stages of sleep, each characterized by particular physiological

Dreams and Sleep

activities and brain rhythms. During the first fifteen minutes, the sleeper descends progressively through each of these stages, before spending about one hour in Stage 4, the deepest level. After this, there is an ascent back up to Stage 1, and it is at this point that the first REM period of sleep begins, usually lasting for about ten minutes. Thereafter, the process of descent and ascent is repeated between four and seven times, although sleep rarely again reaches a state as deep as Stage 4. Each REM episode becomes progressively longer, and the final REM period can last as long as forty minutes.

During REM sleep, brain activity, adrenaline levels, pulse rate and oxygen consumption come closest to those in wakefulness, yet muscle tone relaxes and the sleeper may prove particularly difficult to arouse. It is during REM sleep that most dreaming takes place.

Researchers have found that REM deprivation appears to lead to daytime irritability, fatigue, memory loss and poor concentration. Volunteers who were deprived of REM sleep by being aroused whenever they entered the eye activity phase caught up on subsequent nights by engaging in more REM sleep than usual. It seems that we may badly need REM sleep, and this could be associated with a psychological need to dream.

Recent research has shown that dreams occurring during REM sleep are more visual in content than those that occur at other stages of sleep. Findings even indicate that the eye movements that take place in REM sleep may be synchronized with dream events, suggesting that the brain does not distinguish between the visual imagery of dreams and that of waking life. The same may be true of the brain's response to other dream sensations: stimuli such as a sudden sound or a brief flash of light may be incorporated into a dream and "rationalized" in some way to fit in with its content.

Dreams and Sleep

Dreams and Sleep

However real dream experiences may seem, something prevents us from acting out the actions that fill our dreams. There is a general loss of muscle tone during REM sleep, and the eye muscles appear to be the only ones that are physically involved in acting out dream events. It has been shown that when dreams are at their most vivid, certain inhibitors are produced to prevent muscles from receiving the relevant impulses from the brain, thus ensuring that we do not act on sensory stimuli experienced in the dream. It is perhaps this effective paralysis that gives rise to the dream sensations of attempting in vain to scream, or of trying to walk but being stuck in sand or water. The brain somehow prevents us from moving physically when asleep with the power and agility possessed by the dreaming mind.

★ BETWEEN SLEEPING AND WAKING

Framing the vivid intensity of REM dreaming, our sleep begins and ends with dream images that visit the mind on the boundaries between sleep and wakefulness. Frederick Myers, one of the pioneer British explorers of the unconscious, gave the term *hypnogogic* to the dreams that precede sleep and *hypnopompic* to the dreams that come just as we are awakening.

As the dreamer falls asleep, the brain produces the steady alpha rhythms that characterize a state of deep relaxation; the pulse and breath rate slow down and the body temperature drops. Then the alpha rhythms begin to break up, and the sleeper enters fully into Stage 1 sleep where his or her mind is briefly filled with weird, hallucinatory dreams that characterize the hypnogogic state. Visions may be a better word for them than dreams, for they lack the narrative complexity

Between Sleeping and Waking

and the emotional resonance of dreams in deeper stages of sleep.

Recent research on hypnogogia has centred on its visionary quality. As well as the characteristic scenery, objects and characters of REM-type dreams, hypnogogic images include formless shapes such as waves of pure colour, designs and patterns, and writing, sometimes in foreign, ancient and even imaginary languages. Archetypal faces swim in and out of view, comic and cartoon characters appear and disappear, and images are sometimes presented upside down, or reversed, as if in a mirror.

Hypnopompic experiences share many of the characteristics of their hypnogogic counterparts and often actually briefly persist into wakefulness. Some writers speak of waking from hypnopompic dreams to see figures dancing around the bed or of finding an alien, surreal landscape stretching from their bedroom window. Many have also spoken of auditory rather than visual hallucinations in both hypnogogic and hypnopompic states. Voices warning of impending disaster, mysterious snatches of dialogue or bars of enchanting music are heard as clearly as if they come from within the room. Tactile and olfactory sensations are also common.

Much recent research has attempted to explain the hallucinatory and some-times trance-like nature of the hypnopompic and hypnogogic states by exploring the role that the ego plays as consciousness drifts between waking and sleep. It has been suggested that visionary hypnogogic dreams are a product of the ego's attempt to regain control over thought processes after the rapid change in consciousness caused by the loss of contact with waking reality.

The American psychologist Andreas Mavromatis suggested that both hypnopompic and hypnogogic experi-ences act as anxiety reducers, drawing the dreamer away from the trials and tensions of waking life, and thus serving

Between Sleeping and Waking

29

to promote personal growth and development. By avoiding the narrative and emotional complexity of REM dreams and instead loosening the usual restrictions upon thought, they allow the dreamer to survey the contents of his or her unconscious. By comparing, contrasting and sorting the wealth of material stored in the mind, these processes engender creative insights which flash as if from nowhere into consciousness.

LUCID DREAMING

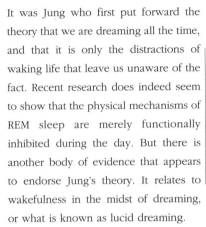

It was Jung who first put forward the theory that we are dreaming all the time, and that it is only the distractions of waking life that leave us unaware of the fact. Recent research does indeed seem to show that the physical mechanisms of REM sleep are merely functionally inhibited during the day. But there is another body of evidence that appears to endorse Jung's theory. It relates to wakefulness in the midst of dreaming, or what is known as lucid dreaming.

The British dream researcher Celia Green has pinpointed several key differences between lucid and non-lucid dreaming. Lucid dreams appear to be free from the irrationality and narrative disjointedness of the non-lucid state, and are sometimes remembered with remarkable precision. During lucid dreams, the dreamer may have access to all the memories and thought functions

Lucid Dreaming

of waking life, and may feel no real difference between sleeping and waking. Above all, the dreamer is aware that he or she is dreaming.

Lucid Dreaming

Usually, something inaccurate or illogical in a conventional dream suddenly alerts the dreamer to the fact of dreaming. The accompanying surge of excitement makes the experience unmistakable. Colours assume a vivid brightness, and objects stand out with a clarity that surpasses our perception of waking experience. Perhaps most remarkable is the dreamer's ensuing ability to control dream events, deciding where to go and what to do, and to experiment with the dreaming environment.

Yet intriguingly, the dreamer can never totally control a lucid dream. The decision, for example, to visit a tropical island in a dream may be the dreamer's own, but the island on arrival will prove every bit as novel and surprising as any seen for the first time in waking life.

In lucid dreaming, the conscious and unconscious minds seem to communicate and co-operate effectively with each other. In bringing the lucid dream under conscious control, the dreamer reaches deeper levels of self-knowledge.

By being aware of, and even dictating, the course of a dream, the dreamer may consciously decide to face the fears and desires that reside there. Rather than running away from a dark force in a dream, lucid dreamers are able to summon such demons, then confront them, aware that because they are only dreaming there is no real need for fear. By confronting the demons in the unconscious, the dreamer not only lessens the terror that they are able to exert, but

Lucid Dreaming

Lucid Dreaming

may also harness the energy of which he or she was previously afraid.

Allied to lucid dreaming, and perhaps a half-way house to it, is the dream experience known as false awakening. False-awakening dreams are also imbued with a vivid clarity, yet the dreamer is not aware of dreaming, but believes that he or she is awake, and may dream in great detail of getting up, washing, having breakfast and setting off to work, only to wake up properly a little while later and have to repeat the whole process for real.

Lucid dreaming has been of valuable assistance to researchers trying to solve the problem of whether dream events occupy a normal time span or whether they condense time. Findings by Stephen Laberge at the University of Stanford, California, in which lucid dreamers carried out previously agreed eye movements to signify their progression through a series of pre-arranged dream events, suggests strongly that dream time approximates to real time.

PRECOGNITION
AND ESP

Belief in the predictive power of dreams is as old as written history. In many ancient cultures, a dream that warned of impending flood, invasion or pestilence would be treated with great solemnity. Thus forewarned, a dreamer might succeed in averting the catastrophe by rescheduling the battle, or, like Noah, building an ark to survive the flood.

The legacy of European scientific rationalism has filled many of us today with a deep scepticism, yet stories of predictive dreaming remain relatively common, especially with regard to the dreamer's own family or friends. But it was not until the work of John William Dunne that any consistent attempt to examine whether dreams can provide glimpses into the future was published.

In 1902, Dunne, a British aeronautical engineer, had a dream that successfully foretold the eruption of Mount

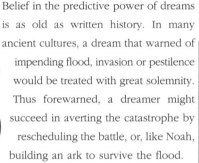

Pelée in Martinique. In his dream, he warned the French authorities that the volcano was about to explode, telling them that 4,000 lives would be lost. Subsequently, he was amazed to read in a newspaper that the volcano had indeed erupted. The headlines, however, told of 40,000, not 4,000 deaths, and Dunne was later to conclude that it was not a vision of the volcano itself that had alerted him to the disaster, but a precognitive experience of reading the newspaper story and of misreading the headline.

A further series of precognitive dreams convinced Dunne that coincidence was no explanation for the frequency and sometimes detailed accuracy of his premonitions. He believed that in dreams we are able to wander backward and forward through time, a theory he expounded in his book, *An Experiment with Time*, published in 1927.

In 1971, two scientists, Montague Ullman and Stanley Krippner, working with the Maimonides Dream Laboratory team in New York, devised a method to investigate precognitive dreaming under laboratory conditions. They worked with Malcolm Bessant, a gifted English sensitive. Before going to sleep, Bessant was told that he would be exposed to a "multi-sensory special waking experience" the next day, chosen at random by the researchers. He might be shown a fire, for example, or given some chocolate to

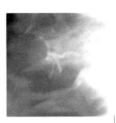

eat while listening to a particular symphony. Bessant was woken up after each REM period to record what he had just dreamed, and independent judges matched his dreams to the "special waking experiences" that followed them.

These experiments were remarkably successful. Of the twelve projects that the Maimonides team completed between 1966 and 1972, nine yielded positive results. During the course of the 1970s and 1980s, the same team also carried out a number of experiments to test more general forms of ESP in dreams, such as telepathy and clairvoyance, using famous art prints as a focus. An "agent", located in a separate room or building from the subject, would concentrate upon one of these images in an attempt to "transmit" it to the dreamer and incorporate it into his or her dream. Again, the results were highly impressive: psychologists declared an accuracy rate of 83.5 per cent for a series of 12 of these experiments.

Researchers have collected a number of clairvoyant dreams apparently related to the sinking of the *Titanic*. Similarly, a retrospective appeal in the British press for dreams connected with the tragedy at Aberfan, a coalmining town in Wales where an avalanche of coal waste buried 140 people alive, produced impressive results. This led, in 1967, to the establishment of the British Premonitions Bureau and the American Central Premonitions Registry.

Dreams of the death of loved ones are even more common. One of the best-known was that of the explorer Henry Stanley, who, after his capture at the battle of Shiloh during the American Civil War, dreamed in detail of the unexpected death of his aunt some 4,000 miles away in Wales. Abraham Lincoln famously dreamed of his own death in 1865, only a matter of days before he was indeed assassinated by John Wilkes Booth.

LEVELS
OF MEANING

An understanding of the structure of the mind's levels is vital
for dream interpretation. The
best model is still the four-fold hierarchy
based on the theories of Freud and Jung.

The conscious mind is governed by
the *ego* – the "I" which can act in the
outside world. The conscious is the
rational, self-aware aspect of the mind.

The preconscious contains material
accessible to the conscious mind upon
demand, such as facts, memories, ideas
and motives.

The personal unconscious stores half-
forgotten memories, repressed traumas
and emotions, and unacknowledged
motives and urges. This is what Freud
called the *id*, which he saw as the primitive, instinctive side of ourselves, and
which must be controlled by the ego.

The collective unconscious is a
genetically inherited level of the mind

containing a mental reservoir of ideas, symbols, themes and archetypes (see pages 65–77) that form the raw material of many myths, legends and religious systems.

There are also three main classes of dreaming, each related to one of the three subconscious levels of the mind:

Level 1 is the most superficial class, drawing primarily upon material in the pre-conscious mind. Dream images from this level can often be taken at face value.

Level 2 deals with material from the personal unconscious, using mainly symbolic language specific to the dreamer.

Level 3 contains what Jung called "grand dreams". These deal with material from the collective unconscious, operating only in symbols and archetypes.

THE NATURE OF DREAMING

Are dreams a revelation from some profound creative source within ourselves, or the confused residue of thoughts and images left over from our waking life?

It is only in the West that we have made determined attempts to dismiss the value of our dreams. Science has so far failed to come to a full understanding of even the theatre in which dreams are acted out – namely, sleep itself.

Since the discovery of REM (Rapid Eye Movement) sleep in 1953 (see page 23), scientists have taken dreams into the laboratory, analyzing them with some of the aids of modern technology. Yet the question posed by Freud and Jung in the first half of the century remains largely unanswered: do we dream to preserve our sleep, or sleep so that we can dream?

Although scientists tend to agree that there must be a purpose to dreaming, they differ over what this purpose might be. The view to which most dream interpreters subscribe is that dreams alert us to important aspects of the state of our unconscious minds.

Freud believed that dreams are coded messages devised by the unconscious to tell of the repressed desires and instincts that dwell there. Jungians go beyond this, recognizing a collective and creative sub-level (the collective unconscious: see page 57) that is vital to our well-being and generates not only the images of our dreams but also those of myth, legend and religious teachings. These theories are the twin cornerstones on which the ideas in this book are built.

It is worth pausing at this point to test the strength of the "psychic garbage" approach, which asserts that we dream to sort and discard our unwanted mental detritus in sleep, and that although the function of dreaming is important, the content of dreams is not.

There are several compelling objections to this approach. First, dream content is not meaningless. Dreams have been shown to provide vital insights into both psychological and possibly physical health, and they can also be an invaluable aid to problem solving. Although they may appear at first to be confused and random, detailed analysis by an expert can show that they contain a wealth of meanings related to the dreamer's circumstances. There is no evidence that people who recall and work with their dreams are any less healthy psychologically than those who do not – in fact, the reverse seems to be true.

No-one who maintains a dream diary (see pages 223–5) over a reasonable period of time should have any difficulty in recognizing that dreams have a remarkable coherence as a secret history of the self.

The Nature of Dreaming

Yet if dreams do contain important messages from the unconscious to the conscious levels of the mind, why is it that we forget much of what we experience in sleep? There are several theories about this, one of which has to do with the manner of our waking. We no longer wake up suddenly as our primitive ancestors did, alert to the dangers of living in the open: instead, we emerge gradually from sleep in the safety of our beds, and it is possibly this which consigns most of our dreams to oblivion between sleeping and waking. Another theory is that we simply sleep too much, and the hours that we spend in dreamless sleep may smother the memories of our dreams.

It may be that the cluttered, distracted and undisciplined nature of our minds also inhibits dream recall. Adepts of the Hindu and Buddhist esoteric orders are said to enjoy unbroken consciousness throughout their sleep, largely as a consequence of their intensive training in techniques of concentration and meditation. They claim to remember their dreams because they are not only conscious of them while they are taking place but also in control of the direction that they take.

According to Freud, "dream amnesia" is directly caused by what he called the *censor*, a repressive ego defence mechanism that protects the conscious mind from the mass of disturbing images, instincts and desires that inhabit the depths of the unconscious.

Dream research requires only a notebook and pencil for writing down dreams, an alarm clock for those who have difficulty with dream recall, and some guidance on dream interpretation. Armed with these minimal resources, all of us can explore deeper and deeper into our dream world, and reach our own conclusions as to the function and value of dreams in our life as a whole.

The Nature of Dreaming

FREUD ON DREAMS

Sigmund Freud (1856–1939) began his classic work *The Interpretation of Dreams* with what was for 1899 a revolutionary statement: "I shall bring forward proof that there is a psychological technique which makes it possible to interpret dreams." Modern dream psychology was born.

Freud trained in Vienna as a medical doctor. His later neurological work convinced him that many neuroses lie below the level of the conscious mind. He undertook a lengthy course of self-analysis in order to explore further this area of the mind and, as a result, became convinced of the role that dreams can play in providing access to material hidden there.

Underlying Freud's dream theories was his belief that the mind processes its material at different levels. He distinguished between the "primary process" which operates in the unconscious, dreaming mind, and the "secondary process" that characterizes conscious thought.

Freud believed that the primary process turns unconscious impulses, desires and fears into symbols; these are linked by associations that have no regard for categories such as time and space, or right and wrong, as the unconscious is unaware of the logic, values and social adaptations of conscious life.

The secondary process, on the other hand, works by subjecting thoughts to the laws of logic, like a sentence that is governed by the rules of grammar.

He maintained that unconscious instincts dwell in a kind of primitive chaos, each seeking gratification independently of the others, and in an animalistic and amoral way. He used the term *id* (literally, "it") to describe the primary part of the mind, and argued that it contains primordial instincts, such as the instincts for self-survival and for the survival of the species.

In Freud's view, the id dominates unconscious life, and dreams are the acting out in fantasy form, or the wish-

Freud on Dreams

50

fulfilment, of its desires and energies. Yet dreams do not emerge directly from this mass of anarchic instincts. If they did, they would arouse the dreamer with their disturbing, often antisocial, and potentially psychologically harmful content. They therefore express themselves only in symbolic form.

In waking life, the ego, the rational part of the mind that is grounded in commonsense reality, and adheres to an acquired moral sense, keeps the id's primitive urges at bay. In sleep, however, the ego relaxes its conscious control, and the id comes to the fore, flooding our mind with its mischievous agenda. To protect the sleeping ego from being disturbed by this inundation to the point where the dreamer is awakened, a mental device that Freud termed the censor struggles to translate the id's material into a less disruptive form. The purpose of dreaming is therefore to preserve sleep by symbolizing dream content in a way that renders it innocuous to the censor.

For Freud, dreams always have a *manifest* and a *latent* content. The manifest content is what the dream appears to be saying, often a jumble of apparent nonsense, while the latent content is what the unconscious is really trying to communicate to consciousness.

The manifest content has two major methods of disguising latent content in a way that can evade the censor. The first is *condensation*: the fusing of two or more dream images to form a single symbol. For example, Freud often interpreted images of older men in his patients' dreams as a condensation of their fathers, on the one hand, and of Freud himself, their analyst, on the other. Working by association rather than by logical connections, the manifest content amalgamates the two images to reflect a similarity in our attitudes toward them both.

The second major device used by the dreaming mind is *displacement*. Like condensation, displacement works by association, translating one dream image into another. When one of Freud's patients dreamed of a ship in full sail, its bowsprit jutting out before it, Freud had no difficulty in interpreting this as a displacement image, the ship standing for his patient's mother, the sails representing her breasts and the bowsprit symbolizing the penis that his patient always imagined his forceful mother to have.

Free association was the method developed by Freud to bypass the condensations and displacements of manifest content in order to arrive at an interpretation of dreams. By following the chains of free association that start from an individual dream image, either we continue wherever our train of thought leads us, or we stop abruptly when we meet resistance, a sudden blockage in the mind that usually reveals the nature of the unconscious problem.

Another important idea in Freud's interpretative method is *secondary revision*. This term describes the way in

Freud on Dreams

which we alter the events and images of our dreams either when recounting them to someone else or when trying to remember them ourselves.

Freud's theory that all dreams originate from the primal chaos of the id was strongly opposed by those who believed that dreams may be simply a continuation of the mind's daytime thoughts, or reactions to recent real-life events.

Accordingly, in the 1920s, Freud modified his views in order to draw a distinction between what he called dreams from "above" and those from "below". Dreams from below arise from the unconscious and "may be regarded as inroads of the repressed into waking life", while those from above result from the day's events, "reinforced [by] repressed material that is debarred from the ego [that is, material unacceptable to the ego, and thus repressed in the id]".

Freud believed that much of our conscious behaviour is also prompted by the need to satisfy unconscious urges.

During the day, we channel instinctive energy into socially acceptable forms, using such ego defence mechanisms as repression, denial and projection in order to keep painful material out of conscious awareness. The ego continually strives to persuade the id that its drives are not going unheard by consciousness as a whole. If the ego should fail in this task of placation, or of maintaining its defences against the id's more disturbing onslaughts, the pent-up instincts and buried traumas of the unconscious can break through into our conscious minds, leading to full-scale mental breakdown.

Even if we escape such a fate, we may waste a great deal of our energy in conflicts between the ego and the id, leading to the obsessions, depressions and anxieties that constitute neurosis.

However, with the help of a psycho analyst, we can avoid such conflicts and strip the id of much of its power. Freud saw the interpretation of dreams as essential to this task.

Freud on Dreams

JUNG ON DREAMS

Carl Gustav Jung (1875–1961), the founder of analytical psychology, spent most of his life working in private psychotherapeutic practice at Kusnacht on Lake Zurich, Switzerland. Like Freud, with whom he worked closely from 1909 to 1913, he believed in the role that the unconscious plays in neurosis and psychosis, and in the important part played by dreams in uncovering the sources of unconscious problems.

Jung departed from Freud, however, in his realization that the common themes running through the delusions and hallucinations of his patients could not all emerge from their personal unconscious conflicts, but must stem from some common source. His extensive knowledge of comparative religion, mythology and symbol systems such as alchemy, convinced him that similar common themes run across cultures and down the centuries, leading to him propounding his belief in the collective unconscious – a genetic myth-producing level of the mind common to all men and women, and serving as the well-spring of psychological life. Jung gave the term *archetypes* to the mythological motifs and primordial images that emerge from the collective unconscious. He saw these as making symbolic appearance over and over again in the great myths and legends of the world, and in our deepest and most meaningful dreams.

When Jung rejected Freud's theory that life energy is primarily sexual, the implications for dream interpretation were profound. Jung saw the sexual symbolism that emerged in dreams as symbolic of a deeper, non-sexual level of meaning, while Freud interpreted the sexual content literally. For Jung, "grand" dreams (those stemming from the collective unconscious) were not coded

Jung on Dreams

messages alluding to particular desires, but gateways to "the vast historical storehouse of the human race".

Jung also rejected Freudian free association, because it allows the mind to follow a chain of association that often leads far away from the original dream image. Jung favoured direct association, in which the analyst concentrates upon the dream, preventing the client's train of thought from wandering by returning it again and again to the original image.

For Jung, psychotherapy is a process of discovery and self-realization. Jungians believe that by being in touch with the mythic themes of our collective unconscious, we gradually integrate the disparate and sometimes conflicting aspects of our selves, developing our full potential as we pass through life's successive stages.

Jung favoured the *amplification* of dream symbols, drawing out their deeper meanings by placing them in their wider mythic and symbolic contexts. Jung's exhaustive analysis of dream material revealed "the numerous connections between individual dream symbolism and medieval alchemy". Alchemy was a precursor of the modern study of the unconscious, and of techniques for transforming the dross, or base matter, of psychic conflict and confusion into the gold of personal wholeness.

Jung not only drew parallels between dream symbols and their alchemical counterparts, but also found in alchemy a symbolic representation of the very process of Jungian analysis and the development of the human psyche. In their search for the powers of self-transformation, alchemists strove to unify opposites such as white and black, heat and cold, life and death, male and female, thus creating the Philosopher's Stone, the single unifying principle.

Jung found in these symbolic alchemical transformations a complex metaphor for the union of male and female, Anima and Animus, conscious and unconscious, matter and spirit that, in his view, led to wholeness within the human psyche itself – a process described by Jung, borrowing an alchemical term, as *individuation*.

Jung saw each stage of life as carrying developmental significance, and stressed the capacity for growth and self-actualization even into advanced old age. The aim of psychotherapy, and thus of dream analysis, was to give the individual access to the personal and collective unconscious, to discover and integrate each aspect of the self into psychic wholeness. In the course of such integration, men and women reconcile not only hitherto conflicting sides of themselves, but free an often repressed *religious function*. Jung discovered through his work with the dreams and neuroses of his clients that this function is at least equal in strength to the Freudian instincts of sex and aggression. The religious function has nothing to do with creeds and dogmas, but is an expression of the collective unconscious that inspires spirituality and love.

CASE FILE I

Freud had the following famous dream in 1895, and it was the first that he submitted to detailed interpretation. It concerned Irma, a young widow and family friend whom he was treating for "hysterical anxiety".

The dream: Freud dreamed that he reproached Irma for rejecting his "solution" to her anxiety problems: "if you still get pains, it's really only your fault". She complained bitterly of "choking" pains in her throat, stomach and abdomen. Alarmed, Freud examined her throat and found a large white patch and "some remarkable curly structures", similar to "bones of the nose". Dr M. repeated the examination and confirmed Freud's findings. Freud decided that the infection was caused by an injection, administered by Otto, a doctor of his acquaintance, probably with an unclean syringe. In Dr M.'s opinion, Irma would soon contract dysentery and the toxin would be eliminated.

The interpretation: Freud saw this dream as a wish-fulfilment. In the dream, Freud first blames Irma for her pains, representing his hidden wish to escape responsibility for the failure of psychoanalysis, and his fear that he has been confusing psychosomatic and physical problems. In his dream world, Irma's "pains" were not caused by his handling of her psyche but by an unclean syringe Otto had used on her. Freud's anxiety about his own treatment of Irma was symbolized by the part played by Dr M., to whom Freud had once made an appeal when his own unwitting mistreatment of a patient had led to her fatal illness. The white patch on Irma's throat reminded him of diphtheria and of the distress caused when his own daughter had the disease; while the nasal-like bones recalled his worries over his own use of cocaine.

CASE FILE II

Jung had this dream when he was trying to establish a relationship between archetypal dream symbols arising from the collective unconscious and the medieval symbolic system of alchemy.

The dream: Jung had had a series of dreams in which a new wing had been added to his house. He had never been able to enter it. One night, however, he passed through the double doors into the wing and found himself in a zoological laboratory resembling his dead father's workroom. Surrounding him were hundreds of species of fish preserved in bottles. He saw a curtain billowing and behind it found his dead mother's bedroom, empty except for rows of what seemed like small floating pavilions, each housing two beds. A door opened into a vast, luxurious hall in which a brass band played loud tunes and marches. The jollity and worldliness were at odds with the sombre atmosphere of the first two rooms.

The interpretation: Many of Jung's "grand" dreams took place in a dream house. By finally gaining access to a new wing in his house, he was symbolically entering areas of his mind that had previously remained unexplored.

The wing consisted of two distinct parts. The laboratory and bedroom represented the hidden spiritual side of himself, which was further symbolized by the many fish, an ancient symbol of Christ. Beyond the curtains, where his own Shadow (see pages 71–74) potentially lurked, the bedroom contained floating pairs of beds – symbols of the alchemical *coniunctio*, the mystical male-female union within the self that leads to inner wholeness. The second part of the wing, consisting of the hall with its loud band and ostentation, represented the conscious mind, the rational world of daylight.

THE LANGUAGE OF ARCHETYPES

The Language of Archetypes

According to Jung, archetypes are the common themes that emerge from the collective unconscious and reappear in symbolic form in myths, symbol systems and dreams. In most instances, archetypal dreams leave us feeling that we have received wisdom from a source outside what we commonly recognize as ourselves. Whether we describe this source as a reservoir of spiritual truth or as an untapped dimension of our own minds, is of less importance than that we acknowledge its existence.

In our "grand" dreams, archetypes appear as symbols, or take personified form as the particular gods and goddesses, heroes and heroines, fabulous beasts and powers of good and evil that are most familiar to our conscious minds. Jungians stress, however, that we should never identify with individual archetypes, because each is only a fragment of the

The Language of Archetypes

complete self. By integrating the many archetypes of the collective unconscious, Jungians hope to progress towards individuation (see page 60).

Archetypal dreams are most likely to occur at important transitional points in life, such as early schooldays, puberty, adolescence, early parenthood, middle age, the menopause, and old age. They also occur at times of upheaval and uncertainty, and mark the process toward individuation and spiritual maturity.

However, Jung cautions that if archetypal dreams contain potent material that appears greatly to contradict the ideas and beliefs of the dreamer's conscious mind, or that lacks the moral coherence of genuine mythological material, then a division may exist between the collective unconscious and the dreamer's waking life. Such psychic blocks must be dealt with before further progress is possible.

Dream archetypes are vital to the search for our "true selves". By looking out for them in dreams, and learning to

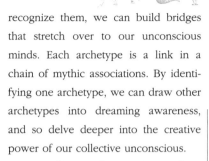

recognize them, we can build bridges that stretch over to our unconscious minds. Each archetype is a link in a chain of mythic associations. By identifying one archetype, we can draw other archetypes into dreaming awareness, and so delve deeper into the creative power of our collective unconscious.

According to the Jungian analysts Edward Whitmont and Sylvia Perera, we know that we have entered the world of archetypes if our dreams confront us with elements that are rationally impossible in everyday life, and that lead us to "the realms of myth and magic". Most dreams reflect the constraints of waking reality, but the moment that we find ourselves in a shape-shifting world in which animals talk, men rise unscathed from mortal wounds, strangers enter through locked doors, and trees twine themselves into beautiful women, we know that we are in the presence of archetypal powers.

Archetypal dream images and events often appear to have a predetermined,

The Language of Archetypes

dramatic power. The dream may be set in a historical or cultural environment far removed from that of the dreamer, symbolizing the fact that he or she is travelling outside the boundaries of waking sensory and psychological experience. It has also been found that archetypal dreams convey a sense of great significance to the dreamer, prompting him or her to see in them "some suggestion of enlightenment, warning, or supernatural help". Above all, archetypal dreams have about them what Jung called a "cosmic quality", a sense of temporal or spatial infinity conveyed by dream experiences such as movement at tremendous speed over vast distances, or a comet-like flight through space, an experience of hovering far above the earth, or a breathtaking expansion of the self until it transcends its narrow individuality and embraces all of creation. Cosmic qualities can also emerge in our dreams as astrological or alchemical symbols, or as experiences of death and re-birth.

Many archetypal dreams involve magical journeys or quests which often, like the quest for the Holy Grail, represent a search for some aspect of ourselves. Such quests usually symbolize a journey into the unconscious, where the dreamer seeks to find and assimilate fragmented parts of the psyche in order to achieve a psychological confidence and wholeness that can differentiate him or her from collective society. Other archetypal journeys, such as sea voyages toward the rising sun, can represent re-birth and transformation.

One archetype with a profoundly numinous quality is the Spirit, the opposite of matter, sometimes manifested in dreams as an impression of infinity, spaciousness, invisibility. The Spirit may also appear as a ghost, or as a visit from the dead, and its presence often indicates a tension between the material and non-material worlds. Other major Jungian archetypes are described on the following pages.

The Language of Archetypes

SEVEN MAJOR ARCHETYPES

THE WISE OLD MAN

The Wise Old Man (or Woman) is what Jung called a *mana* personality, a symbol of a primal source of growth and vitality which can heal or destroy, attract or repel. In dreams this archetype may appear as a magician, doctor, priest, teacher, father, or any other authority figure, and by its presence or teachings convey the sense that higher states of consciousness are within the dreamer's grasp. However, the *mana* personality is only quasi-divine, and can lead us away from the higher levels as well as toward them.

THE TRICKSTER

The Trickster is the archetypal antihero, a psychic amalgam of the animal and the divine. Sometimes seen as an aspect of the Shadow (opposite), the Trickster appears in dreams as a clown or buffoon, who while mocking himself at the same time mocks the pretensions of the ego and its

Seven Major Archetypes

archetypal projection, the Persona (see below). He is also the sinister figure who disrupts our games, exposes our schemes, and spoils our dream pleasure. The Trickster often turns up when the ego is in a grim situation of its own making, through vanity, over-arching ambition or misjudgment. He is untamed, amoral and anarchic.

THE PERSONA

The Persona is the way in which we present ourselves to the outside world in waking life. Useful and non-pathological in itself, the Persona becomes dangerous if we identify with it too closely, mistaking it for the real self. It can then appear in our dreams as a scarecrow or a tramp, or as a desolate landscape, or as social ostracization. To be naked in dreams often represents loss of the Persona.

THE SHADOW

Jung defines the Shadow as "the thing a person has no wish to be". He identified the shadow as the primitive, instinctive

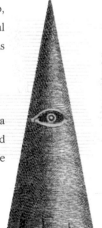

Seven Major Archetypes

71

side of ourselves. The more we repress this side and isolate it from consciousness, the less chance there is of preventing it from "bursting forth suddenly in a moment of unawareness".

Concealed under a civilized veneer, the Shadow reveals itself in the selfish, violent and often brutal actions of individuals, communities and nations. In dreams, the Shadow usually appears as a person of the same sex as the dreamer,

often in a threatening, nightmarish role. Because the Shadow can never be totally eliminated, it is often represented by dream characters who are impervious to blows and bullets, and who pursue us into the eerie basements of the mind. However, it can also take the form of a sibling figure, or a stranger who confronts us with the things we prefer not to see and the words we prefer not to hear.

Because the Shadow is obsessional, autonomous and possessive, it arouses fear, anger or moral outrage in us. Its appearance in dreams indicates a need for a more conscious awareness of its existence, and for more moral effort in coming to terms with its dark energies, which otherwise gradually overpower the conscious mind. We must learn to accept and integrate the Shadow because the unpalatable messages it gives us are often indirectly for our own good.

THE DIVINE CHILD

The Divine Child is the archetype of the regenerative force that leads us toward individuation: "becoming as a little child", as it is expressed in the Gospels. It is therefore the symbol of the true self, of the totality of our being, as opposed to the limited and limiting ego. In dreams, the Divine Child usually appears as a baby or infant. It is both innocent and vulnerable, yet at the same time inviolate and possessing great transforming power. Contact with the child can strip us of any sense of personal aggrandisement, and reveal to us how far we have strayed from what once we were and aspired to be.

THE ANIMA AND ANIMUS

Jung believed that we each carry within us the whole of human potential, male and female. The Anima represents the supposedly "feminine" qualities of moods, reactions and impulses in man, and the Animus the supposedly "masculine" qualities of commitments, beliefs and inspirations in woman. More importantly, as the "not-I" within the self, the Anima and Animus serve as *psychopompi*, or soul guides, to our unacknowledged inner potential.

Mythology represents the Anima as maiden goddesses or women of great beauty, such as Athena, Venus and Helen of Troy; the Animus is symbolized by noble gods or heroes, such as Hermes, Apollo and Hercules. If Anima or Animus

Seven Major Archetypes

appear in our dreams in these exalted forms, or as any other powerful representation of man or woman, it typically means that we need to integrate the male and female within us. If ignored, these archetypes tend to be projected outward into a search for an idealized lover, or unrealistically ascribed to partners or friends. If we allow them to take possession of our unconscious lives, men can become over-sentimental and over-emotional, while women may show ruthlessness and obstinacy.

THE GREAT MOTHER

The Jungian image of the Great Mother plays a vital role in our psychological and spiritual development. Its prevalence in dreams, myths and religion is derived not only from our personal experiences of childhood, but also from the archetype of all that cherishes and fosters growth and fertility on the one hand, and all that dominates, devours, seduces and possesses on the other.

Not only is the energy of the Great Mother divine, ethereal and virginal, but it is also chthonic (generated from the earth) and agricultural – the earth mother was worshipped as the bringer of harvests. Always ambivalent, the Great Mother is an archetype of feminine mystery and power who appears in forms as diverse as the queen of heaven and the witches prevalent in myth and folktale.

For Freud, the symbolic dream-mother reflected the dreamer's relationship with his or her own mother. Freud observed that most dreams involve the dreamer, a woman and a man. He believed that the woman and man often represent the dreamer's parents, and maintained that they symbolize aspects of the Oedipus and Electra complex from which men and women respectively suffer. (From Greek myth, Oedipus symbolizes the early male sexual desire for the mother and jealousy of the father. Electra represents the early female desire for the father and jealousy of the mother.)

✦ CASE FILE III

The dreamer is a university professor. He is currently trapped between maintaining his academic reputation, and risking it by openly declaring his growing interest in mysticism and spiritual growth.

The dream: "After swimming in the sea I went to take a fresh-water shower on the beach. The water ran over my back, but before I could rinse my front, I suddenly found myself in a smart drawing-room where I dripped water on the carpet. There were several middle-aged women there who looked at me disapprovingly, and a much younger one with a mandolin

who said: 'Don't worry, music can always dry you.' Then I floated up onto the roof. It was night-time; I stretched out a hand and for a moment held a star in my hand. A voice said: 'Put it under your chest.' I was trying to fathom out how to do this when I suddenly woke up."

The interpretation: Swimming in the sea indicates the dreamer's desire to travel deeper into the archetypal unconscious. However, he then tries to wash the salt-water away – he wishes to "sanitize" whatever insights he has discovered.

The transition to the drawing-room reminds him that he cannot be his true self in an artificial environment, especially under the disapproving gaze of his colleagues (the middle-aged ladies). The musician's words are those of the archetypal Anima, telling him that his creative energies can transform the wisdom of the unconscious into the spiritual realm of air.

He then floats up to the roof, where he can see the stars, archetypes of higher states of consciousness. But on waking he still cannot understand how to put a star "under his chest", and so integrate his higher self fully into his conscious life.

Case File 999

DREAM SYMBOLS

When we wake in the morning, it is often the bizarre nature of our dream memories that convinces us of their unimportance. Yet once we learn to interpret dream symbols, a new dimension of meaning is opened up.

Symbols are the "words" used by dream language: each one represents an idea, a memory, a mood arising from the dreamer's unconscious. However, many dream symbols can change their meaning from one participant to another.

In every sense, dreaming represents a personal language between the unconscious and the conscious mind, and although we can learn the typical meanings of many dream symbols, we can never be sure that we have understood them until we have worked upon them in the light of our unique experience. The most apparently trivial symbol may unlock the most potent memory or the most telling piece of advice.

Generally, Level 1 and 2 dreams, which arise respectively from the preconscious and the personal unconscious (see pages 41–42), make most use of symbols that carry particular associations for the dreamer, or that arise from the general currency of everyday life. Many of these have elements of common usage; others may make sense only to the dreamer.

Although making sense, a Level 1 or 2 symbol may carry sufficient emotional charge to be used only in the dreams of particular people. For example, rage may be symbolized for one dreamer by a farmer, because it was a farmer who once threatened to shoot him for trespassing; while for another dreamer it may take the form of the puzzle that once drove her to the limits of frustration.

Level 1 and Level 2 symbols can also be taken from more peripheral aspects of life, such as TV programmes. The dream plunders the dreamer's memory, choosing the motifs that most readily serve its purposes.

Dream Symbols

Symbols in Level 3 dreams usually carry a much more universal meaning. Not only are the archetypes (see pages 65–77) common to us all but so are the forms in which they typically arise into awareness. The problem with Level 3 dreams often has to do with the reluctance of our modern Western consciousness to recognize that dreams can help us contact a reservoir of wisdom frequently beyond the range of our waking minds.

Freud and Jung disagreed over what is meant by a symbol. Freud assigned a fixed meaning to dream images. For him steeples, guns, knives, doors, caves and the like all represented sexual objects, whenever they appeared in dreams. For Jung, however, this was to treat images as signs and not as symbols. Jung maintained that the substance of a symbol "consists of our unconscious contents that make themselves felt, yet the conscious is unable to grasp their meaning". A sign, on the other hand, represents a fixed interpretation of a dream image, and therefore one restricted to a meaning that is already conscious. Treating a dream image as a sign not only denies us access to its deeper meaning, but further represses that meaning and thus widens instead of narrowing the gap between the conscious and the unconscious.

For Freud, a phallic symbol represented a penis; for Jung, it was "the creative *mana*, the power of healing and fertility". Most psychologists and anthropologists who have studied symbols favour Jung's more creative approach.

A symbol can carry a variety of meanings. Thus, under analysis, the image of a gun may emerge even for the same dreamer as representing thunder and lightning, male procreation, destruction, and the toy the dreamer wielded as a child. These meanings show respectively that power can be used to destroy, to do good, to do evil, or to reinforce a childish urge to intimidate others.

Dream Symbols

PERLS ON DREAMS

The American psychiatrist Fritz Perls (1893–1970) is best known as a founder of gestalt therapy, which emphasizes the way in which the individual organizes the facts, perceptions and behaviour that make up his or her life, rather than the separate nature of each.

Like Jung and Freud, Perls stressed the symbolic content of dreams, but he also believed that every character and object in our dreams is a projection of our own self. For Perls, dreams represent unfinished emotional business, and their symbolic content stems from the dreamer's personal experience.

Role play, Perls believed, is a more efficient and accurate technique for interpretation than either free or direct association. His method was to ask the dreamer to dramatize each dream image in turn, giving voice even to inanimate dream objects, and sometimes adopting the physical positions that such objects had in the dream, to best represent what message they were trying to convey. Role play of this kind places interpretation firmly in the dreamer's hands. The therapist may make suggestions, but meaning must never be imposed from outside.

Jung and Freud also emphasized that dream images often symbolize aspects of the dreamer's own self, and that role-play exercises can be a helpful addition to direct or free association. As valuable as Perls' methods are for working with Level 1 and Level 2 dreams, they risk undervaluing the shared meaning of dream symbols and, in particular, of ignoring the role of the collective unconscious.

Perls on Dreams

BOSS ON DREAMS

The Swiss psychiatrist Medard Boss (1903–1990) posited a relationship between dreaming and existentialism. Existential theory argues that each individual chooses consciously or unconsciously what he or she wishes to be. Thus, for Boss, dreams are not a profound symbolic language, but represent straightforward aspects of existential choice.

In clinical practice, Boss showed that dreams can provide psychological help without being interpreted symbolically. In place of association, he developed an interpretative method which allowed Level 1 dreams to tell their own story.

In one dream experiment, Boss hypnotized five women – three healthy and two neurotic – and suggested that each of them dream of a naked, sexually aroused man known to be in love with them and advancing on them with sexual intent. While the three healthy women followed the given scenario exactly and enjoyably, the dreams of the two neurotic women were anxious and unarousing. In one of them the naked man was replaced by a uniformed soldier armed with a gun with which he nearly shot her. Boss pointed out that there was nothing symbolic about the first three dreams. They were simply expressions of the dreamers' conscious desires. And even the dream of the soldier simply reflected the woman's fear of men.

However, Jungians and Freudians would point out that, under association, the elements that arose from the dreamer's unconscious (lover transformed into soldier, penis into gun) could give insights into the causes of the woman's neurosis.

Boss on Dreams

THE INNER LANGUAGE

Before Freud and Jung, most scientists argued that dreams were nothing but a random jumble of meaningless images left over from the sensory accumulation of our daily lives. During this century, inspired by Freud's assertion that dreams, in their own way, have meaning, psychologists have proposed numerous, often conflicting, theories to explain the logic they employ.

The often bewildering nature of this logic reflects the dreams' origins outside the tidy confines of the conscious mind. A dream can be a response to events in the outside world, or it can originate within, expressing aspects of the dreamer's deep-seated preoccupations and feelings; it can be a means of fulfilling desires or of highlighting unresolved emotions in the dreamer's everyday life. Often enigmatic, halting and fragmentary, the language of

The Inner Language

dreams can warp time, mix the familiar with the unknown, and work fantastic transformations by its own brand of psychic "magic". In the dream world, one scene merges into another, inanimate things move of their own accord, and may talk, and even become intensely threatening. People or animals may fly, or a person may bark like a dog, or walk naked in a crowded place. The meanings dreams hold have to be teased out from such complex and contrary happenings.

The following pages form a "traveller's guide" to the most significant aspects of the dream world, from the logic of dream sequences to the enchanted landscapes that characterize children's dreams and nightmares.

Dream Logic

Until the revolution in dream theory brought about by Freud and Jung, few philosophers disagreed with the nineteenth-century German physicist Theodor Fechner's assertion that in dreams "it is as though psychological activity has been transported from the brain of a reasonable man into that of a fool". What disturbed philosophers was not only the apparently "nonsensical" content of the dream images themselves, but also the apparent absence of rational thought and higher mental functions in the logic that links dream images together.

However, Freud observed that connections between things can be demonstrated by means other than words – as is the case, for example, with art. He believed that "the madness of dreams may not be without method, and may even be simulated, like that of the Danish prince [Hamlet]". Although dream connections do not follow the

rational logic of language and philosophy, it is possible that they adhere to a more oblique rationale in order deliberately to disguise the meaning of the dream.

Clinical experience showed Freud that dream images interconnect by means of linking devices. The first is *simultaneity*, when images or events are presented together. The second is *contiguity*, when

Dream Logic.

dream images or events are presented in sequence. Thirdly, there is *transformation*, when one image dissolves into another. And lastly, *similarity*, which Freud considered to be the most frequent and important linking device and which operates through association, as when one object resembles another in some way, or recalls or invokes feelings about that second object. Many of these associations are forgotten or repressed at a conscious level, making the connections harder to unravel, but they can be revealed through appropriate techniques of dream interpretation. By deciphering them, the psychoanalyst lays bare not only the operation of dream logic but also its profound subtlety.

Dream researchers since Freud have identified *internal consistency* as playing a key role in the operation of dream logic. Analysis of Level 1 and 2 dreams (those that are generated by the preconscious and personal unconscious) shows that each dreamer may well have his or her own particular way of manifesting this consistency.

The most common form which consistency takes, labelled *relative consistency* by the dream researchers Calvin Hall and Vernon Nordby, lies in the frequency with which various dream images appear to individual dreamers over a period of time. Thus, furniture, body parts, cars and cats may appear in descending order of frequency for one dreamer, while for another subject, women may appear more often than men and outdoor settings more often than indoor. From one year to the next it has been shown that these frequency patterns remain remarkably constant.

Another important form of internal consistency in dreaming is *symbolic consistency*. When using symbols, the dream selects them solely on the basis of their associations with the material to be expressed, and repeats the more successful ones in dream after dream to get its message through.

Dream Logic

DREAM SCENERY

Dreams are most often set in familiar locations, reflecting the immediate interests and memories of the dreamer and imbued with all the resonances of his or her social and cultural background. Research has shown the house to be the most common setting; however, as demonstrated by Jung's dream which helped to inspire his theory of the collective unconscious, the most apparently mundane scenery can carry a remarkable depth of symbolic information.

The house that featured in Jung's dream represented his own psyche. Its various floors led progressively deeper into his unconscious until he arrived at the "primitive man" who inhabited the cellar. Jung subsequently encouraged his followers to examine the dream scenery that featured in their dreams at progressively deeper levels in order to reveal its symbolic meaning. A house, for example, may

be taken progressively to signify the dreamer's body, his mind, his mother's body, and even – by a common process of dream punning – his father's family or "house". Generally, the more creative and imaginative the dreamer, the more likely it is that such progressive levels of meaning will emerge, and that the dream scenery itself will be varied, colourful and striking.

Many artists have been inspired by the scenery of dreams. Painters such as the Italian Surrealist Giorgio de Chirico (1888–1978) and the Belgian Surrealist Paul Delvaux (1897–1994) are particularly credited with capturing the dream atmosphere. It is the juxtaposition of the ordinary and the extraordinary, captured in their paintings, that gives dream scenery its special quality, and that invests nightmares with their chilling power.

As with the more obvious, foreground elements in a dream, an item of dream scenery can suddenly transform itself. A carpet may turn into a swamp, a

Dream Scenery

Dream Scenery

distant farm may turn into a slaughter-house. By means of these reversals, the nightmare startles the mind out of conventional habits of thinking so that deep emotions and anxieties are exposed.

Dream landscapes are often deeply experienced, rather than merely observed. A landscape may ache with loneliness, or be suffused with a mysterious sense of well-being. If the landscape has gentle contours and evokes strong feelings, one possible interpretation is that it symbolizes the body, especially the mother's body. Dream places can also represent the topography of the mind itself: for example, a strange neighbourhood in a remote part of town can be a symbol of the unconscious. Nocturnal scenes can suggest the murky depths of the inner self.

It is vital, during interpretation, to remember the details of the dream landscape if the full meaning of the dream is to be revealed. If a scene is set in a garden, is it formal or informal in design, well-kept or overgrown? If there is a road, does it wind and double back upon itself, or is it long and straight, an easy journey home?

Even those parts of the scenery that appear to be merely backdrops can have a significance which may emerge as central when analyzed by techniques such as those of Fritz Perls, including dramatic enactment by the dreamer of each remembered aspect of the dream (see pages 84–85). Because any element in the scenery can also represent a different person or a different aspect of the dreamer's personality, it is important to establish, if possible, what relationship each element has to the dreamer. Does the dreamer own the setting, or does it have associations, however strange, with someone of his or her acquaintance? What emotion does the scenery arouse? If it could speak, what would it say?

The more closely we attend to dreams, the more vivid dream scenery becomes, and the more powerful a vehicle of dream consciousness.

Dream Scenery

CASE FILE IV

The dreamer is a male sales executive. He has always wanted to be a novelist, but now spends much of his time writing misleading but effective publicity material.

The dream: "I was in a hairdressers' awaiting my turn. The salon was small and dark and rather seedy. There were two men ahead of me, sitting on my right, with their heads in their newspapers, but the hairdresser called me first. It seemed that he knew me, and that I had been there before.

"I was rather put out by this, and thought that he wanted to ingratiate himself with me. When I went to sit in the chair, however, I found that I was in the salon on my own. The mirror in front of me was so old I was unable to see myself reflected in it. Then I was outside, looking into the windows of some stores. I think that I was trying to find some scissors to cut my own hair, but was unsuccessful."

The interpretation: The dreamer associated his dream trip to the hairdresser with ineffectual vanity, and the hairdresser's ingratiating behaviour with the way in which others lavish praise and attention where it is not due, a situation that he clearly associated with his work.

The presence of the men who should have been called before him indicates that there are deeper, still mute and latent aspects of his self, such as his gifts as a writer, which should be given priority.

The mirror in which the dreamer could not see his face was a reminder that he had allowed his self-knowledge to decay in the environment of falsity in which he currently worked. His search in store windows indicated that he was trying to satisfy his needs by looking for opportunities outside himself.

CASE FILE V

The dreamer is a woman in her late twenties who holds a responsible and challenging executive position with a firm of real estate agents in a big city.

The dream: "This is one of a series of dreams in which I find myself surrounded by old and broken objects, or new gadgets that, whatever I do, somehow refuse to work.

"In this dream, I found myself standing at the top of a long flight of steps. They seemed to lead down to a backyard full of rubble and scrap metal, yet the steps themselves were wide and grand, rather like those in the garden of a chateau.

"I could see a man in the scrapyard working on an old car. I asked him why it wouldn't go. He said it worked now, because he had fixed it."

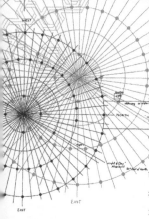

Case File 09

The interpretation: Steps downward usually represent a way into the personal unconscious. The steps in this dream appear to lead to the broken, discarded rubbish of old memories and useless objects. However, the man working among the junk in the backyard signifies that psychological healing and creative activity continue in the unconscious mind, even though we are usually unaware of them, and that what may seem like psychic rubbish can be of great value, if we approach it in the proper way.

He tells her that he has "fixed" the old car, a means of travelling, of getting somewhere, and perhaps in this case symbolic of a disappointed aspiration or ambition in the dreamer's earlier life.

The dreamer considers that her dream is telling her that she must act with more trust and courage in her attempts to journey into the world of the unconscious. If she does so, her inner life may become clearer to her.

CHILDREN'S DREAMS

We are born dreamers. We may even dream in the womb and certainly spend much of our early life in dreams. About 60 per cent of the sleep of newborn babies is passed in the REM (Rapid Eye Movement) state (see page 23) where most dreaming occurs.

Although it is obviously impossible for us to know exactly what small babies' dreams contain, it is probable that much of their dream content is triggered by physical sensations, or consists of dreams about physical sensations. After the first month of their lives, visual

and auditory images probably also begin to play a part.

Once children are old enough to tell us about their dreams, the

content primarily reflects their waking interests and emotions.

Robert Van de Castle and Donna Kramer of the University of Virginia analyzed many hundreds of dreams from children aged between two and twelve, and found that from an early age, girls' dreams were longer than those of boys, and contained more people and references to clothes, while boys dreamed more about implements and objects. Animals featured much more prominently in children's dreams than in those of adults, and the ratio of frightening animals such as lions, alligators and wolves to non-frightening animals such as sheep, butterflies and birds was far higher. This frequency of animal images would seem to reflect children's basic interests, and the way in which animals symbolize their wishes and fears.

Children report around twice as many aggressive acts in their dreams as do adults. Occasionally, children play the role of aggressors, but more often they are victims, and fear has thus been shown to be their most common dream emotion.

Robert Kegan, a North American developmental psychologist, has suggested that this high level of aggressive acts represents the difficulty that young children have in integrating their own powerful, spontaneous impulses into the social order and control demanded of them by adults. The wild animals, monsters and bogeymen of children's dreams also seem to symbolize children's inner awareness that such impulses lurk just below the conscious surface of their behaviour and may break out and wreak havoc in the conscious mind if self-control is relaxed.

In psychoanalytical theory, as well as representing aspects of the dreamer's self, the bogeymen of children's dreams can also symbolize parents and other powerful adults. A young child has problems in consciously reconciling the

loving, providing aspects of a mother or father with their function as agents of discipline and fear. Dream witches and wolves are thus ways of representing and accepting parents' punitive role, while the child's own acts of aggression toward parental symbols in dreams can symbolize their wish to be free of the dominating force that adults exercise.

Freud believed that a child's relative lack of sexual desire simplifies the nature of their wish-fulfilment, leaving the way clear for the desire for food to assert itself. Jungian psychology, however, claims a level of interpretation for children's dreams that goes beyond that of wishes and desires, recognizing in the bogeyman, hero and heroine the archetypal images already activated in the child's unconscious, and symbolizing not only aspects of waking life but also the child's mystical sense of his or her own inner nature.

Children's Dreams

CASE FILE VI

The dreamer is an eight-year-old girl who is having problems with her teacher at school. This dream took place after a school trip to a science museum, which the teacher claims the child did not enjoy.

The dream: "There was a big truck with a boiler thing behind it outside the school, and my teacher said she thought it was going to explode. A man got out of the truck and came toward me, and I was frightened and ran away. Then I was in the car with my Daddy, and we were driving away from this man, and my Daddy went through a red stop light.

Then someone said that the thing had exploded, and my Daddy said we must go back to the school and see what it was that had happened. But I didn't want to go back there."

The interpretation: The threatened explosion outside the school is clearly associated with the teacher, and may represent what appears to the child as the teacher's unpredictable outbursts of anger. The threatening man may symbolize the fear she has of her teacher. The girl relies on her father to make good her escape, but knows that he can only do so by breaking the rules of the adult world, jumping a red stop light. But as soon as he hears of the teacher's anger (the explosion) he decides that they must return to school. Although she "didn't want to go", she realizes that she must learn to accept the sometimes unpredictable and frightening aspects of the adult world that her teacher symbolizes.

Case File 09

109

CASE FILE VII

Case File VII

The dreamer is a female athlete noted for her determination on the track, but whose relationships and social life have always been troubled and unsatisfactory.

The dream: "It was summer and I was standing on an open road stretching into the distance. I saw someone approaching in the distance, and realized at once that though they were running they were moving in terrifying slow-motion. I was rooted to the spot and everything went deathly cold. Then somehow I was sitting on the back of a horse, but it just kept eating the grass, and refused to move. Then I was suddenly off the horse and chasing someone, determined to catch them and teach them a lesson for giving me these nightmares. The creature ran into a room at the end of a corridor, and I thought, 'Now I've got you'; but when I ran into the room the

door slammed and locked behind me, and the creature turned a horrible face toward me and screamed in triumph."

The interpretation: As an athlete, the dreamer can usually "solve" her problems by running faster than her opponents, but in her anxiety dream nothing allows her to escape, even though the "someone" who menacingly approaches her is moving deliberately slowly. She interpreted this as representing her feelings of powerlessness when dealing with other people, a powerlessness the causes of which she must try hard to identify.

The horse may represent the natural force of her emotions, which is unable to take her along the stretch of open road toward a secure relationship.

She interpreted the terrible final scene, in which she is trapped in a locked room, faced by the "horrible" demon of her own anxiety, in these words: "It means I lead myself into my own difficulties; I am my own worst enemy."

Case File VII

DREAM
DIRECTORY

Dreams are the conversations that we have with ourselves. They take the form of a symbolic language that sends messages between our unconscious and conscious minds. We are the authors and actors of our dreams, and the best judges of their meanings.

In Level 1 and 2 dreams (see page 42), which arise from the personal unconscious, the dreaming mind communicates through the use of symbols that carry particular associations for the dreamer, mostly originating in recent waking events. This directory is intended as a starting point to stimulate interpretation of such dreams, so that we can understand the wealth of imagery available to the dreaming mind.

Level 3 dreams, from the collective unconscious (see pages 42 and 57–58), find their associations in

a wider pool of archetypes (see pages 65–77). Jung used amplification (see page 58) to tease the meanings from the imagination.

The first part of this Directory is organized according to underlying themes. The second part examines common dream phenomena and offers possible explanations for them. After studying the Directory, you may find that your dreams begin to use these themes as a language your conscious mind can understand.

THEMES

🍂 CHANGE AND TRANSITION

Our conscious minds are often unaware of the psychological and emotional upheavals that follow major changes in our lives. However, the unconscious tends to know better. If in our unconscious minds we are nervous

Change and Transition

TRANSFORMA-
TIONS
During a dream, a change from autumn and winter to spring and summer may indicate deep inner transformations within the dreamer. A bridge can symbolize change, spanning the boundary between the past and future, suggesting the opportunities available on the other side.

and insecure in the face of change, our dreams may be filled with comforting images of our former ways of life and most familiar surroundings. The dreaming mind may also show its anxiety about a particular transition by an exaggerated sense of strangeness, perhaps imbued with feelings of dread.

More usually, our dreams advise us of the desirability and inevitability of

OBJECT COMING
TO LIFE
If an inanimate object comes to life in a dream, it may be that previously unac-knowledged inner potential is ripe for development.

UNFAMILIAR
SURROUNDINGS
If unfamiliar sur-
roundings make
the dreamer feel
lost or afraid, he
or she may not
yet be ready to
leave an old way
of life behind.
However, feelings
of excitement
suggest that the
dreamer is ready
for change.

change. They may indicate which direc-
tions we should take, warning us of
potential pitfalls, or providing encour-
agement during the transition period.

The need for change may appear in
dreams as the act of redecorating our
homes or changing our clothes, or buying
new books or CDs to replace old ones.
Dreams of crossing a road, river or bridge
may indicate the risks that change may
bring, or symbolize its irrevocable nature.

DIRECTION AND IDENTITY

If we are afraid of losing direction in our lives, this may give rise to dreams in which we are trapped in fog, or wandering in an unfamiliar landscape. If our dream journey is fraught with anxieties, we may not be ready to leave the secure confines of the conscious mind, and should take stock before approaching the "true self". However, if the route in the dream becomes increasingly clear, and the goal is excitedly anticipated, it may be time to tread a new path.

Provided that we can read it, a chart or map symbolizes a sure direction; if it is incomprehensible, however, our loss of bearings may be followed by frustration and panic. In dreams, the map can represent self-knowledge, and a failure to read its signs warns us that we are in danger of becoming unknown territory to ourselves.

CAR LOSING CONTROL
Anxiety about a loss of direction in life may cause dreams of hurtling out of control in a car or train.

MASKS
If the dreamer is unable to remove a mask, or is forced to wear one, this suggests that their real self is becoming obscured.

Fears about loss of identity may give rise to dreams in which the dreamer is unable to recall his or her name, or is unable to produce important identification documents when they are demanded.

Direction and Identity

STRANGE REFLECTIONS
It can be very alarming to look into a dream mirror and see someone else's face there. This is the classic dream to represent an identity crisis, the sudden sense of not knowing who we are.

ity

Direction and Identity

Direction and Identity

MAZES

A maze in a
dream usually
relates to the
dreamer's
descent into the
unconscious. It
may represent
the complex
defences put up
by the conscious
ego to prevent
unconscious
wishes and
desires from
emerging into
the light.

SUCCESS AND FAILURE

As in our waking lives, success and failure are among the most common preoccupations of our dreams. Whatever our anxieties, we often believe in our hearts that failure can be overcome; more certain still is the knowledge that success is usually short-lived. When

warring against the Greeks, the Persian prince Xerxes dreamed of a crown of olives whose branches spread out over the world but then suddenly vanished – an accurate omen that his conquests would soon be lost. However, most dreams of success or failure are linked less to actual events than to the dreamer's state of mind.

Dreams of failure often contain situations such as

PRIZES
In dreams, even if the nature of a prize or trophy is obscure, the sense of triumph associated with it is obvious.

knocking on a door without reply, or finding oneself without money to pay for a taxi or settle a debt, or losing a contest or an argument. Success in dreams may be indicated by a favourable outcome to a transaction, often accompanied by feelings of fulfilment or even elation. A fence or hurdle commonly stands for a particular challenge confronting the dreamer in waking life. Jumping over the obstacle may represent not only the possibility of success but also the confidence upon which that success may depend, and which the dreamer must strive to acquire. Level 3 dreams (see page 42) sometimes reflect success at a deep level of personal growth and transformation.

WINNING
A RACE
This indicates
a recognition
of the potential
within ourselves.
To come second
or third may
suggest aspira-
tions beyond
one's abilities.

Success and Failure

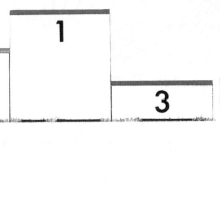

123

COMMUNICATION BREAKDOWN Failure to make oneself heard, or otherwise to give a good account of oneself, strongly suggests feelings of inadequacy, and the dream indicates the need to confront them in waking life. Failure to make oneself understood on the telephone can suggest weaknesses in the dreamer's ideas or in the ability to convey them convincingly to others.

ANXIETY

Anxiety

Anxiety is probably the most common emotional state expressed in our dreams. In sleep, our fears often rise into awareness, filling our dreams with unsettling, highly charged symbols, and with dark, troubled moods. Such dreams not only indicate how deeply rooted our anxieties can be, but they also remind us of the need to tackle the source of these worries, either by confronting a specific external challenge or by learning to be less fearful of life's predicaments.

Anxiety dreams are recognizable by the emotional charge that they carry. Typically, the dreamer has the sensation of trying to cope with several duties simultaneously, or of trying to complete a never-ending task. Other anxiety dreams include crawling through a narrow tunnel (often believed to represent birth anxiety), or being choked by smoke. If anxiety stems from social inadequacy, the dream may involve public embarrassment, such

FALLING
Falling from a great height may emphasize that the dreamer has climbed too high in personal or professional life and is now ready for a fall.

BEING CHASED
Dreams that involve being chased by an unseen but terrifying presence usually indicate that aspects of the self are clamouring for integration into consciousness.

as grotesque incompetence on a crowded dance floor.

Melodramatic dream events, such as falling into the hands of evil captors, may reflect relatively mundane problems. The point of such extreme forms of terror is to underline the need to bring into consciousness (as a prelude to dealing with them) repressed desires and energies.

Anxiety

FRUSTRATIONS
Being arrested may indicate feelings of guilt. To dream of failing to obtain what we want often suggests a lack of communication between the conscious and unconscious.

TRYING TO RUN
Trying to run in a dream but finding one's legs are rooted to the spot, or moving in painfully slow motion may result from mechanisms in the brain that prevent us from acting out our dreams while we are asleep.

DROWNING
Dreams of drowning, or of struggling in deep water, may represent the dreamer's fear of being engulfed by forces hidden in the depths of the unconscious mind.

WELL-BEING AND OPTIMISM

Well-being and Optimism

An optimistic or happy dream can occur at any time, even when we are feeling the full weight of life's burdens. Such dreams may leave us exalted and content, not only with our own lives but also with the world as a whole.

Optimistic dreams may contain symbols of good luck or peace – either images that are personal to the dreamer, such as a lucky stone or colour, or cultural symbols of good fortune, such as black cats, doves or olive branches. Some people interpret these dreams as being prophetic of future success; others believe that they show that the journey toward fulfilment has begun.

HONEY AND BEES
Bees in dreams were long regarded as auspicious symbols, predicting peace and prosperity.

LIGHT

The appearance of light in dreams is thought to confirm that profound insights are illuminating or about to illuminate the conscious mind of the dreamer. Through amplification of these dreams, the dreamer may find religious associations, for example with Christ as the light of the world.

Dreams that present configurations of the dreamer's lucky number are usually a cause for optimism. More potent still are dream visions of the rainbow, the archetypal symbol of hope and reconciliation. The gate is an enduring symbol in dreams of an entry into a new world of opportunity and enlightenment.

Lucid dreams (see pages 31–34), which are generally characterized by feelings of joy and excitement, often contain particularly vivid and stimulating colours.

When worked on through amplification (see page 58), dreams indicating well-being and optimism may produce associations with the Elysian fields, the paradise of classical mythology.

Well-being and Optimism

COLOURS

Bright or vivid colours often indicate the onset of a "grand dream" (see page 42). Orange symbolizes hope.

AUTHORITY AND RESPONSIBILITY

People in positions of authority and responsibility in waking life often report dreams that reflect their status. Such dreams may involve episodes such as dealing with emergencies or receiving requests for decisions from all sides.

On occasions, authority and responsibility dreams merge into anxiety dreams. The dreamer may seem to be giving orders which no-one obeys, or suffering a sudden rejection at the hands of superiors. Such images draw attention to the dreamer's feelings of insecurity, and indicate the need to become more fully

WEARING
A TALL HAT
Crowns and tall hats are traditional symbols of authority, raising the wearer above his or her peers and colleagues.

integrated into his or her public role. Authority and responsibility dreams may also reveal frustrations and resentments felt about the over-dependency of other people: such dreams fulfil a dual purpose by allowing these feelings harmless expression and by drawing attention to the over-stretched role that the dreamer is being called upon to play in waking life.

Many people dream of sitting at the head of a long table. The longer the table, the more people the individual at the head has under his or her command. Rejection of the food by those sitting at the table suggests disagreement with the dreamer or a refusal to accept his or her authority.

STACKS OF PAPER
To dream of a desk stacked high with an unending pile of paper is a typical anxiety dream for those in authority. The dream may help the dreamer to see that he or she is not dealing effectively enough with incoming work.

Authority and Responsibility

RELATIONSHIPS

When analyzing dream relationships, it is particularly important to remember that the dreaming mind is intent not upon duplicating reality but, rather, upon commenting on reality. It thus frequently uses dream characters as symbols rather than as depictions of actual people with whom the dreamer is involved in waking life.

As revealed by direct association, a complete stranger in a dream may represent characteristics of a wife or husband, while a partner may stand for some aspect of the dreamer. The dream is therefore more concerned with its message than with portraying people as they really are. Thus, in the course of dream analysis, a friend transformed into a stranger may reveal a fundamental ambivalence in the dreamer's general feelings about friendship. Sudden rejection of a loved one may indicate the dreamer's rejection of some part of his or her own nature. Separation from one's

MENDING THINGS
Repairing an appliance such as a radio often indicates the need to work at a relationship to stop it from deteriorating. An appliance that has been unaccountably dismantled may also carry this meaning.

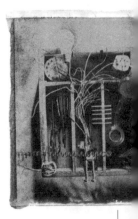

children may suggest the loss of cherished ideals or the failure of personal ambitions.

At other times, dream characters do indeed seem to represent themselves, but they do so in order to draw attention to unrecognized aspects of our relationships with them. Frequent dreams of family

members may show an over-dependence upon the family. New parents often dream of accidently rolling upon a baby in the bed, and are probably expressing in dream symbolism their anxiety about their new nurturing role.

Failure to make a telephone connection may suggest loss of intimacy in a

BIRDS
Blackbirds represent jealousy. Magpies may suggest aspects of the self stolen by a partner.

HOTELS
In dreams, hotels often represent impermanence, a point of transition in a relationship, or even a loss of personal identity.

relationship, while dreams of intense heat or cold may reflect burning passion or cool indifference toward a partner.

During amplification, symbols from a Level 3 dream (see page 42) may provide associations with mythical themes such as the love between the Egyptian

FIRE
This is a powerful and ambivalent dream symbol. Fire destroys, but it also cleanses and purifies. In dreams it can signal a new beginning, or represent disruptive emotions – perhaps the flames of passion or envy.

FEATHERS
Feathers often represent the dreamer's desire to show warmth or tenderness to someone close to him or her.

deities Isis and Osiris. Isis, the ancient Egyptian symbol of motherhood, is said to have loved Osiris even in the womb.

Another archetype sometimes revealed through amplification is the witch, symbol of the terrifying role of the Great Mother (see pages 76–77), and established in fairy tales worldwide. Rather as the witch can symbolize the destructive aspect of the Mother, the giant or ogre can symbolize that of the Father.

GOLD DUST
To dream of gold dust running through one's fingers can signify regret at the ending of a close personal relationship (or of any other specially cherished experience).

SPIDERS
In dreams, the devouring mother, who consumes her children through possessiveness or her power to arouse

guilt, is often symbolized by the spider. The web woven by the spider to ensnare its prey is also a common dream image.

Relationships

135

SEXUALITY

For Freud, unconscious sexuality lay behind much of our conscious behaviour; he saw sexual imagery as the main driving force of dream symbolism.

Freudians often associate mutilation with castration, and beating oneself or others with masturbation. Riding a horse or bicycle, or chopping wood, or taking part in any rhythmical activity, connotes sexual intercourse. The same meaning is attributed to climbing stairs or a mountain, the crashing of waves on the seashore, travelling, and the insertion of any one object into another, such as a key into a keyhole. Acts of deflation, such as a collapsing balloon, can refer to impotence; locked doors or windows are seen as representing frigidity.

In the Jungian approach, even explicit sexual themes may emerge as symbols of higher creative processes. Cultural precedents for this include the

RED ROSE
In Freud's view, this traditional symbol of love often indicates the female genitalia.

WHIPS
Whips generally represent the dreamer's awareness of power, domination and obedience in relationships.

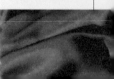

erotic sculptures that adorn the exterior of many Hindu temples, referring not only to the union of male and female but to wholeness within the self and to the marriage between earth and sky, mortal and divine, spirit and matter.

GUSHING WATER

Objects from which water gushes are often symbols of ejaculation. Flowing water may also denote a new burst of creativity.

KNIVES

The knife or dagger is the most common male sexual symbol. It can represent the penis in its ability to penetrate, and can stand for masculinity in its associations with violence and aggression. It may also represent the "sword of truth" that cuts through falsity and ignorance, or the will to cut away false desires.

QUILLS AND CANDLES

Because they stand erect, quills and candles often symbolize the penis. They may appear in dreams as symbols of masculinity.

CUPS

The cup is a classic female sexual symbol. However, because it may contain wine, and through its associations with the Holy Grail, a cup may also stand for love and truth.

VELVET OR MOSS

In Freudian dream analysis, velvet and moss usually represent pubic hair. Other dream interpreters see in them symbols of a more generalized longing for the comforts of nature, or for gentleness, sensitivity or innocence.

HATS AND GLOVES

Because they enclose parts of the body, these are often used by the dreaming mind to represent female genitalia.

PURSES
The purse is among the most common of female sexual symbols. It can stand both for the female genitalia and the womb.

SHOES
Some dreamers associate shoes with sexuality, as they can be entered by other objects, or by parts of the body. Women's shoes sometimes stand for dominant female sexuality.

Sexuality

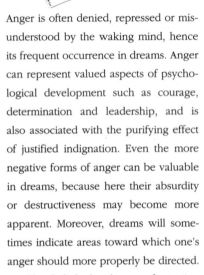

Anger and Frustration

ANGER AND FRUSTRATION

FRUSTRATING
TASKS
In dreams,
apparently mean-
ingless tasks (such
as building a
house of cards)
may eliminate the
tenacious hold
that the ego has
on consciousness
or may remind
the dreamer that
the ability to live
with unavoidable
frustrations is a
sign of maturity.

Anger is often denied, repressed or mis-
understood by the waking mind, hence
its frequent occurrence in dreams. Anger
can represent valued aspects of psychological development such as courage,
determination and leadership, and is
also associated with the purifying effect
of justified indignation. Even the more
negative forms of anger can be valuable
in dreams, because here their absurdity
or destructiveness may become more
apparent. Moreover, dreams will sometimes indicate areas toward which one's
anger should more properly be directed.

Closely linked with anger, frustration
is also commonplace in dreams. We may
find ourselves missing a train or an
appointment, or unable to read an important message. In such instances, the
dream may be reminding the dreamer of
the need to discover the cause of his or
her frustration, or to deal more effectively with it if its causes are known.

BOTTLED-UP FEELINGS

A dream may draw attention to repressed anger or frustration by images such as bottled-up gas, and to unbridled anger by flames roaring out of control. Anger toward particular people may emerge in dreams when the dreamer prepares poison for them, or defaces their photograph.

Anger and Frustration

DAM BURSTING

Anything that suggests a controlling force giving way before fierce energies from within can be a potent image of anger or frustration contained beyond the point of self-control. A flood blocking a pathway may represent the dreamer's frustration, and suggest the need to find an alternative route. In this way, the dreamer is reminded that there is often more than one way to deal with frustrations.

LOSS AND BEREAVEMENT

A LOVED ONE RECEDING
Distance is often used to symbolize bereavement in dreams. A loved one may be seen receding into the distance, or waving good-bye from a far-off hilltop.

EMPTY PURSE
The discovery of an empty purse or pocket may indicate the loss of both a loved one and the security the old relationship offered.

The need to continue with life sometimes means there is insufficient time to grieve over the death or departure of a loved one. In such instances, the dream may do the grieving for us. Images of loss are part of the healing process.

Loss of any kind may be symbolized by the despairing search for a friendly face in a crowd, or by themes of ashes or dust. Dreams may be steeped in nostalgia, providing warm or poignant images of a past way of life or occupation. Some part of the unconscious mind needs to repeat these experiences over and over again as an emotional safety valve until it can finally accept that the loss has really taken place.

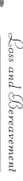

AN UNLIT HOUSE
In dreams, a house often represents the dreamer, or those things that give life its stability and orientation. Empty or dark windows suggest extinction of the loved one and of vital aspects of the dreamer's conscious life.

Sometimes, bereavement dreams look ahead rather than back into the past. The dreamer may see the loved one in happy circumstances, or be visited and reassured by him or her. Such dreams can leave the waking mind with feelings of well-being, even elation, and in many instances are so realistic that the dreamer feels certain of the reality of life after death.

RELIGION AND SPIRITUALITY

Jung saw the search for spiritual and religious truth as one of the strongest energies of the psyche and identified it as emerging directly from the collective unconscious. Religion and spirituality often express themselves in "grand" Level 3 dreams (see page 42). The dreaming mind may encounter the Wise Old Man, or other archetypal figures of wisdom, who reveal their truths and teachings. Other archetypes may take the form of symbols or religious icons. Transcendental experiences may occur, leaving the dreamer with profound feelings of exaltation and inner peace.

Level 1 and 2 dreams (see page 42) often depict the spiritual world in more practical terms. Dreams involving religious officials may

THE BUDDHA
The Buddha's image in a dream often reminds the dreamer of the need to find stillness at the centre of his or her own being.

Religion and Spirituality

represent the authority of the established church, while Christian saints, Hindu *avatar*s or Buddhist *boddhisattva*s may symbolize aspects of the dreamer's spiritual identity or aspirations.

Dreams that we may be tempted to interpret in sexual terms, such as climbing mountains or trees, may actually portray spiritual progress. A church may represent the purified self or the richness and mystery of spiritual teachings. An eagle's flight may signify spiritual aspiration, while a fall to earth could warn against the dangers of spiritual pride.

Amplification of spiritual dreams may focus upon one of the creation or incarnation myths.

SHIVA
The Hindu deity Shiva may appear as the dual aspect of divinity: he is the destroyer as well as the creator.

Religion and Spirituality

VIRGIN MARY

In dreams, the Virgin Mary often represents a supreme and selfless love or compassion, and the power that rules the heavens through grace and sanctity.

BEING OF LIGHT

The being of light is an archetypal image that embodies a universal spiritual principle, relevant to all cultures and all religions.

SYMBOLS

THE BODY

In ancient Egyptian, Greek and Roman and medieval European culture, the body was used as a metaphor for the spiritual world. Dreams may also link the body to the spiritual realm. The bodily condition of the dreamer or of other characters in dreams may reflect traits in the dreamer's psyche, or levels of psychological or spiritual progress.

Dreams make use of bodily symbols because the images are readily understood by the conscious mind. A dream may use the symbol of the eyes to relate it to the inner world of the "soul", or use the metaphor of physical strength to denote the inner world of moral resolve.

The dreaming mind can be highly creative with body metaphors. When we are asleep, our waking feelings of physical modesty and propriety are usually suspended, and our dreams may thus feel free to use symbolism that would normally be disturbing to the conscious mind. For example, as well as erotic images, the dream may show the intestines to symbolize "guts" or courage. And it may use the relationship between the body and the outside world in a symbolic

The Body

LEFT AND RIGHT
For Jungians, the right side of the body in dreams often refers to aspects of conscious life, while the left side is the unconscious.

way – thus, hand-washing may indicate the denial of responsibility, or purification, or signify guilt or immorality.

Dreams may also allude to the body as a warning to attend to health problems, or to express feelings about diet or exercise. For early dream workers, body dreams could reveal the future. Thomas Tryon, a nineteenth-century English dream interpreter, insisted that to dream that one's belly is extended foretells an increase in family or property, while seeing one's back predicts bad luck or the coming of old age.

The Body

BONES
Bones can represent the essence of things. Being stripped or cut to the bone may signify a sudden insight. Broken bones may suggest fundamental weaknesses.

TEETH
Artemidorus interpreted the mouth as the home, with the teeth representing its inhabitants.

Teeth (falling out, broken, and so on) are the focus of many of our anxiety dreams.

HEART
The heart has archetypal significance as the centre of emotional life, and as the symbol of love.

EYES
Eyes are symbolic windows into the soul, and provide clues to the dreamer's state of spiritual health.

MOUTH
For Freud, mouths may represent fixation early in psycho-sexual development.

HAIR
Hair often symbolizes vanity. Ritually shaving the head indicates a renunciation of worldly ways.

BIRTH AND RESURRECTION

The collective unconscious seems not to recognize finality, but projects instead a constant cycle of change. Dreams often enact re-birth and renewal by taking the dreamer back to childhood, overlaying old memories with new experiences. A dream that we are back in childhood may thus reflect adult concerns (such as the need for or the achievement of rejuvenation), rather than a wish to re-visit our formative years. Similarly, if we dream that we are older than we actually are, age may simply be standing in as a symbol for wisdom, or for rigidity, or for infirmity.

Resurrection – the return to life of deceased people, animals or trees – is a classic dream archetype, often associated with new life suffusing old ideas or challenges. Alternatively, such dreams may

FINDING AN EGG
Finding an egg, a baby or any other image of birth can indicate the emergence of new possibilities in the dreamer's waking life.

THE DIVINE CHILD

One of the most powerful archetypal symbols, the Divine Child represents perfection, re-birth and the innocence of primal wisdom. Associated in many spiritual traditions with the virgin birth, the Divine Child may symbolize the dreamer's own spiritual potential, ever-present beneath the dross of worldly concerns.

Birth and Resurrection

warn of the return of problems that have not yet been laid properly to rest.

Birth (often from the dreamer's own mouth, belly or genitals) is frequently associated with new ideas and solutions, sometimes simply as wish-fulfilment, but sometimes as a clear indication of actual possibilities waiting to be explored.

NUDITY AND CLOTHING

Nudity and Clothing

In Level 3 dreams (see page 42), nudity can represent the dreamer's spiritual nature, or the authentic self. In Level 1 or Level 2 dreams (see page 42), it can stand for vulnerability, a desire to shed defences, a freedom from shame, or a love of truth. Excessive anxiety about nudity in oneself or others may suggest a fear of honesty and openness in relationships, or a failure to accept and integrate one's own sexual energies. For Freud, nudity

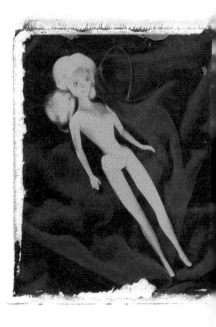

could also represent a longing for the lost innocence of childhood, or an expression of repressed sexual exhibitionism, usually the result of punitive parental attitudes toward the dreamer during the self-display stages of childhood.

THE FEMALE NUDE
Venus and other classical goddesses were often portrayed naked, or almost so. Such divine nudity was used as a symbol of love and sacred beauty.

ACCEPTING NUDITY

To accept others' nudity indicates the dreamer's ability to accept them for what they really are.

NUDITY IN CHILDREN

Nudity in the young usually represents innocence, but can also stand for mischief or love.

INDIFFERENCE

To dream that others are oblivious to our nakedness indicates that we should discard fears of rejection.

Clothing is similarly ambivalent. It can take the form of the brilliant garments of light worn by the saints, gods and angels, or it can stand for earthly vanity, an urge to deceive by appearances or to conceal shame or imperfection.

Although a cover for nakedness, clothes may, by their cut, line or function, draw attention to what they purport to hide. Dreams about brassieres or trousers may therefore represent thoughts about breasts or genitals, or about maleness, femaleness or sexuality.

Clothing, particularly in auspicious colours, may represent

DISGUST AT NUDITY

To be distressed or disgusted by the nudity of another person suggests anxiety, disappointment or aversion at discovering their real nature behind the pretensions of the Persona.

Nudity and Clothing

ARMOUR
To dream of wearing armour indicates that the dreamer is being over-defensive.

positive aspects of the dreamer's psychological or spiritual growth, but when over-elaborate may suggest pretension, or a weakness for worldly display. Because clothes can make the wearer seem taller or thinner, richer or poorer, than he or she really is, they can stand for self-accusations of hypocrisy: a particularly flashy waistcoat or tie may represent our knowledge that we are deceiving others in some way, establishing a persona at odds with reality.

OVER-TIGHT CLOTHES
These usually indicate that the dreamer is inhibited or restricted by his or her public or professional role.

CLOAK
The cloak can stand for illicit concealment and secrecy, for mystery and the occult, or for protective warmth and love.

JEWELS
Gold and diamonds typically represent the true self, while rubies denote passion, sapphires truth, and emeralds fertility.

UNDERCLOTHES
Underclothes may represent unconscious attitudes and prejudices. Their colour and condition indicate the qualities concerned.

OTHER PEOPLE

GIANTS
In adult dreams,
recollections of
childhood may
be represented
by giants.

We meet many other people in our dreams. Some are straightforward representations of people we know, who remind us of our particular preoccupations; others represent, in a more abstract way, particular qualities, wishes or archetypal themes; others stand for aspects of the dreamer's own self. Such is the condensed economy of dream symbolism that a single character can at times fulfil all three functions in the passage of a single dream.

Detailed analysis is often required before the exact function of a dream character can be

THE SHADOW
This archetype
represents all the
dreamer wishes
not to be. It is his
or her darker
side, and sym-
bolizes hidden
or repressed
aspects of the self.

Other People

identified, but certain general tendencies are apparent. Jung established that a dream companion who appears in various guises in several dreams, but is recognized as the same character, represents aspects of the dreamer's real self. By reflecting in waking life upon the behaviour of this character in the various dream circumstances, we are provided with insights not only into the self but also into how the self may appear to others.

THE HERO

Dreams often use fictional characters to convey archetypal messages. The Grail knights, for example, are archetypal Heroes, sacrificing themselves in the service of a higher quest.

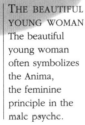

THE BEAUTIFUL YOUNG WOMAN

The beautiful young woman often symbolizes the Anima, the feminine principle in the male psyche.

THE BEAUTIFUL YOUNG MAN

Symbol of the Animus, the masculine principle in the female psyche.

THE SILENT WITNESS

A person in a dream who refuses or is unable to speak often represents an undeveloped function within the self.

HEALTH

The Ancient Greeks and Romans believed that dreams could offer diagnoses and cures. Some recent dream interpreters have said that cures can arrive in dreams if the dreamer has concentrated on the problem before sleeping. For Jung, some dreams give clear messages concerning both physical and psychological health.

FRACTURED LIMBS
These represent a threat to life and to our power.

HOSPITALS
Dreaming of being hospitalized may show a desire to relinquish control over one's own body or a fear of losing this control.

WEIGHT LOSS
Weight loss often represents the draining effect made by people needing a lot of attention.

BODILY FUNCTIONS

Freud associated dreams of excretion and toiletting with the anal phase of psycho-sexual development. The small child experiences erogenous satisfaction from excretion, and this experience, if insensitively handled by adults during toilet training, may leave the individual with permanent feelings of shame, disgust and anxiety over natural functions.

In Freud's view, anal fixation may even account for personality dysfunctions such as miserliness and uncontrollable rage.

LACK OF PRIVACY
If the dreamer fears that a toilet lacks privacy, it may indicate fear of public exposure, or a need for greater self-expression.

TOILET DREAMS
Excretion usually represents the dreamer's public anxiety or shame, or his or her wish to express or unburden the self, whether for creative or for cathartic reasons. Menstruation is often associated with a sudden release of creative energy.

Bodily Functions

MORTALITY

At an individual level, death has always vexed, terrified and fascinated us, and the Level 1 and 2 dreams (see page 42) that lie not far below the surface of our conscious minds may be filled with anxieties about our own death or about the ultimate loss of loved ones or close friends.

Fearful dreams about our own mortality may indicate the need for us to come more to terms, in conscious life, with our inevitable fate. Dreams about the death of others may depict more abstract fears – for example, a concern

Mortality

FUNERALS
Burial may represent the repression of desires and traumas, and may also denote an end, or the need for an end, to a particular phase of the dreamer's life.

about the annihilation of the personality or the self, or a dread of judgment or divine retribution, or of hell, or of the manner of death, and so on. Many dreams of death have no association with mortality at all. Some may relate to aspects of the dreamer's own psychological life, or to a change in life circumstances.

Reading the obituary of someone during a dream, or seeing their tombstone, or attending their funeral, may suggest the dismissal of that person from a job, or their relegation from the dreamer's affections, or their fall from grace in some other way.

SYMBOLS OF DEATH
Skulls, hourglasses and the figure of the reaper are important symbols of death. Dreams of such deathly paraphernalia may remind the dreamer that life carries a limited span in which to complete projects, or may point to forthcoming finalities such as the end of a marriage.

Mortality

CAPTIVITY AND FREEDOM

Dreams often focus on the conflict between the restrictions that life places

upon us and our urge for freedom. Another common theme is our need to dominate others by holding them captive, possessing them or placing them under some kind of obligation to us.

The dreamer's own need for freedom may be symbolized in similar ways, with the dreamer struggling to break free from others. Awaiting execution is a symbol for the most extreme curtailment of freedom, although in dreams it may

BEING TIED UP
Dreams of being tied up may indicate the dreamer's need for freedom, but were seen by Freud as a reflection of repressed sexual fantasies dating back to early childhood.

relate to apprehensions about potentially auspicious events, such as marriage.

Freedom and captivity may also symbolize aspects of psychological life that are being too tightly controlled by the dreamer. Potential abilities that the dreamer is refusing to acknowledge may also be represented by captivity dreams, as may ideals and feelings that are being denied, or the urge to find meaning and spiritual purpose in life.

DOMINATION
Bondage can have erotic overtones or suggest spiritual aspirations.

LIBERATION
This shows an urge to release another from psychological bondage.

Captivity and Freedom

CLIMBING AND FALLING

Logic suggests that climbing dreams indicate success, and falling dreams failure, but other interpretations can reach a deeper level of meaning. For Freud, climbing dreams represented a longing for sexual fulfilment, but they also carry connotations of aspiration in other areas of life, such as personal or professional growth. Falling can symbolize failure or pride, but it can also represent an unsettling descent into the unconscious.

Tripping and falling often emerges as a reminder of a failure to take care of the more basic or emotional aspects of life. Dreamers rarely report distress when hitting the ground: they often wake up just in time or find the ground soft. Such dreams remind us that apparent disasters may often lead to no long-term harm.

Dreams of falling from a rooftop or from a high window usually indicate insecurity in an area of worldly ambition.

ELEVATORS
Elevators usually suggest that the dreamer's ascent or descent is less the result of his or her own efforts than a consequence of chance and the actions of others. In some instances, the elevator suggests the rise of thoughts from the unconscious.

Falling from a burning building may suggest that the dreamer has been under insupportable emotional pressures as a result of his or her aspirations.

SLIPPERY SLOPES
The common dream in which we attempt to climb up a slippery slope or greasy ladder suggests failure to make progress in a desired area.

flying

FLYING

Flying dreams often bring a sense of exhilaration, and some dreamers speak of a strange recognition, as if flying is a skill that they have always possessed, yet have forgotten how to use. Rarely are flying dreams experienced as unpleasant or fearful, and the sense of freedom and exultation that they convey often open the dreamer's imagination to the infinite possibilities of life.

Dreamers do not always fly alone, but may be surrounded by friends or strangers, suggesting that others share their insight into the true nature of things. They may be accompanied by an animal or an object, perhaps symbolizing

FLYING A KITE
To dream of flying a kite emphasizes the controlled freedom of some aspect of the dreamer. Kites can also stand for exhilarating but ultimately unproductive schemes.

AIRPLANE
Flying in a plane can symbolize a wish to travel, a desire for rapid progress, or to succeed in a particular enterprise.

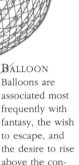

Flying

BALLOON
Balloons are associated most frequently with fantasy, the wish to escape, and the desire to rise above the conflicts of daily life.

FLYING UNAIDED
Flying unaided can be an archetypal expression of the dreamer's higher self, or his or her sense of immortality.

INCONGRUOUS VEHICLES
Flying in a bed or an armchair suggests a desire for adventure tempered by a strong predilection for safety.

important aspects of personal or professional life. Dreamers may find themselves flying in a vehicle of some kind, or they may be leaping into the air on giant strides.

It is rare in dreams for flying to become confused with falling. Usually the dreamer floats gently to earth, having enjoyed panoramic views of the world below.

TRAINS
Trains suggest
that the dreamer
has help on his
or her journey.

STATIONS
AND AIRPORTS
These can
indicate appre-
hensions or
excitement
about the future.

TRAVEL AND MOTION

Freud was convinced that dream events incorporating travel or motion typically represent disguised wish fulfilments for sexual intercourse. However, travel and motion can stand for many other aspects of life, in particular for progress toward personal and professional goals.

Jung noted the appearance in "grand" (Level 3; see page 42) dreams of the archetypal quest for meaning and ful-filment – dreams of setting out on a jour-ney are far more frequent than those of arriving at the journey's end. The dream-ing mind reveals the need for progress in life, but indicates that decisions on ulti-mate goals must be taken at the con-scious as well as the unconscious level.

Much is conveyed by the nature of the dream pathway that stretches ahead. An open road usually suggests new pos-sibilities for progress, while a rocky path may indicate many obstacles. However, dream interpretation sometimes reveals

Travel and Motion

CARS AND BOATS
For Freud, the car symbolized progress in psychoanalysis. Sea travel may represent a journey into the unconscious.

CROSSROADS
These usually represent a point of decision, the coming together of people or ideas, or a parting of the ways.

that a seemingly difficult pathway is nevertheless the one to take. The scenery through which the dreamer is passing also reveals aspects of his or her inner life. To dream of a journey through a desert, for example, may indicate loneliness, aridity, or a lack of creativity.

Further insights come from the means of transport: Jung noted that travelling in a public vehicle often means that the dreamer is behaving like everyone else instead of finding his or her own way forward.

EATING AND FOOD

Eating has always been associated with sexuality, and dreams involving eating and food were long interpreted in sexual terms. However, food and eating demand a wider interpretation than the strictly

MEAT
Freudian psychology suggests that dreaming of eating meat signifies absorbing one's own instinctive energies.

sexual. Bad-tasting food can suggest a sourness in the dreamer's emotional life; waiting in vain for a meal can suggest neglect, emotional disappointment or lack of adequate support. Impressions of having over-eaten can variously

Eating and Food

SOCIAL MEALS
Social meals that carry a positive emotional charge often reflect intimacy with others, shared interests and harmony.

TYPES OF FOOD
As well as sensuality, fruit can represent fertility in the creative arts or science. Milk usually represents kindness, sustenance and nourishment, while luxury foods such as chocolate generally represent self-indulgence.

represent greed, lack of discrimination, sensuality, or short-sighted behaviour. Refusal to accept food may suggest a desire to end dependency upon others, while providing food for others can indicate the urge to give support.

PICNICS
Picnics represent a desire for simplicity.

FASTING AND GORGING
Freud saw the mouth as the primary erogenous zone, and fasting and gorging as a symbol of sexual desire (denied or indulged). Fasting may also stand for self-punishment, perhaps because of guilt.

VACATIONS AND RELAXATION

TROUBLES ON VACATION
These suggest an inability to escape from the responsibilities of normal life.

Most dreams are highly active, and it is rare to find oneself relaxing. However, dreams that symbolize a desire for relaxation are common. Some dreams also recognize that vacations can be stressful – such dreams represent anxieties in other areas of the dreamer's life.

Sometimes the dream contrasts the dreamer's own agitated state with the relaxed behaviour of others, emphasizing the subject's need for stress-reduction. At times, the dreamer may feel irritated by the inactivity of others, and this suggests resentment at receiving insufficient help in waking life, or anger at his or her own impotence.

ISOLATED PLACES
Seeking an island or a deserted place reflects a craving for solitude.

PACKING FOR
A VACATION
Preparations for a
vacation generally
suggest a need
to escape from
everyday prob-
lems, or to seek
new experiences.
A wish to travel
light can indicate
a recognition of
the unnecessary
"baggage" that
we usually carry
with us through-
out life.

At other times we may find that
vacation dreams become confused with
travel dreams of a different kind
(see pages 170–171). For example, what
starts out as a vacation may end
up as a business trip. In such dreams,
the unconscious may be
indicating the dreamer's
inability to relax and
the conscience-stricken
impulse to turn toward
more earnest or dutiful
pursuits as a reward-
ing alternative.

FESTIVALS AND RITUALS

The cultures of the world have always used festivals and rituals to celebrate important recurrent events, to honour the gods, to mark the passage of time and to celebrate transitions in our lives.

Dream rituals invite the dreamer to escape the confines of the conscious mind. Performers may wear masks or special clothes, sing a particular song or recite ritual incantations, leaving their everyday identities behind to enter the archetypal world of the unconscious.

FERTILITY RITES Dream images of these rites often emerge from the collective unconscious. Rituals may involve sacrifice to a harvest deity, representing the death of the past to ensure future fertility and prosperity.

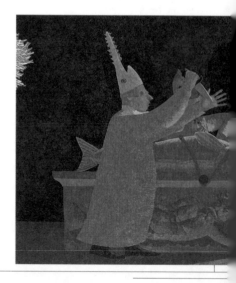

WEDDINGS
A wedding often suggests the union of opposite yet complementary parts of the self, and the promise of future fertility. In Level 3 dreams, it may symbolize the union within the dreamer of male and female, rationality and imagination.

Dreams associated with Christmas or other major religious celebrations can represent peace, generosity, goodwill, family and friends or a confirmation of spiritual truths. Wedding or other anniversaries can serve as reminders of transience, or more positively as indications of the significance of human and family ties, or – if the emotional charge is negative – of the restricting commitments involved. Dreams involving baptisms or christenings frequently represent purification, new beginnings, or the acceptance of new responsibilities.

ROM

ART, MUSIC AND DANCE

In dreams, the arts represent not only the dreamer's personal creativity, but also a link to higher levels of consciousness.

Sometimes we awake from our dreams uplifted and inspired with the dying notes of an exquisite melody in our ears. Such music usually comes from Level 3 dreams (see page 42), and symbolizes the states of mind associated with higher levels of inner development.

The eighteenth-century Italian composer Giuseppe Tartini dreamed that the Devil appeared to him and played such a beautiful solo on the composer's violin that even the inferior copy

MUSIC
Beautiful music in dreams can symbolize the potential of creative life. Discordant music suggests distorted creative potential.

PAINTING
Successful painting can represent the dreamer's creative potential and the rightness of his or her vision of life.

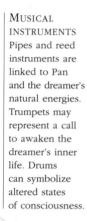

recalled by Tartini upon waking (the "Devil's Trill") is considered by critics to be his best work.

If we dream of giving an artistic performance, this may be emphasizing our own unrealized potential, while being only an observer or listener may suggest a need to draw inspiration from others. Certain instruments, such as the harp, have always symbolized especially celestial qualities, while others, such as wind instruments, have often stood for more instinctive, sensual energies.

Because dreams draw upon the same sources as the imagination, they can provide artistic inspiration, yielding ideas, or sometimes complete pieces.

MUSICAL INSTRUMENTS
Pipes and reed instruments are linked to Pan and the dreamer's natural energies. Trumpets may represent a call to awaken the dreamer's inner life. Drums can symbolize altered states of consciousness.

DANCING
This can represent sexual courtship or sexual intercourse.

PLAY

In dreams, play and games may symbolize work and other serious issues, just as work may emphasize the value of playfulness.

Dreaming of soft toys often represents comfort, security, or uncritical emotional support, which the dreamer may be seeking. Alternatively, the dream may indicate a refusal to face reality, or may be registering a need for more natural or more tactile contact with loved ones.

Play symbols are open to a wide range of interpretation. Freudians, for example, link the rhythmical motion of a swing with sexual intercourse, while others maintain that this can also represent the exciting, unpredictable nature of life, or may be reminding the dreamer of the freedom of childhood. Board games in dreams often represent the dreamer's

DOLLS
Dolls may represent the Anima or Animus, the qualities of the opposite sex within ourselves. Jung also found that dolls can indicate a lack of communication between the conscious and unconscious.

TOY TRAINS
These may represent our wish to assert control over the direction and power of our own life.

progress throughout life, with all its advances and set-backs. They may be wish-fulfilments, in which the dreamer competes and wins, or they may reveal a fear of competition.

Dreams of play often emphasize that the best ideas come when the mind is in a playful, relaxed mood. Conversely, such dreams may suggest that the dreamer is taking serious issues too lightly, or that what seems an innocent diversion may be to others a matter of deep concern. Playfulness may also indicate that we are breaking the rules upon which a relationship or some other important issue depends.

PUPPETS
Glove puppets or marionettes suggest manipulation and a lack of free choice.

Fighting and Violence

Dreams often use physical violence as a metaphor for conflicts of other kinds within the dreamer's own mind. When the dreamer is the victim of violence the dream may represent an assault upon status or relationships, or a threat to finances, health, or general welfare. If the subject enjoys watching

Wars and Battles

Jung believed that wars and battles were a sign of major conflict between aspects of the dreamer's conscious and unconscious minds.

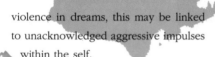

violence in dreams, this may be linked to unacknowledged aggressive impulses within the self.

Violence to the Self

Violence toward the dreamer often represents a desire for self-punishment.

An Impotent Weapon

Any weapon that refuses to fire in defence of the dreamer suggests powerlessness.

Violence to Others

This may represent a fight against unwanted aspects of the dreamer's inner or outer life.

TESTS AND EXAMINATIONS

Dreams about examinations can be highly stressful. Among the most anxious of examination dreams is that in which we arrive to face a test without having done any revision, or find that the paper is written in an incomprehensible language. Dream examinations may stand for success and failure in any area of our personal or professional life. Failure in a dream test can encourage the dreamer to face up to shortcomings that he or she may have been unwilling to see.

Particularly when taking place in cold, impersonal surroundings, an examination can represent the remote powers of bureaucracy and authority that sometimes seem to control the dreamer's life.

Tests and Examinations

INTERVIEWS
The interviewers may represent aspects of the dreamer's self, suggesting self-rejection or self-dissatisfaction.

GIVING AND RECEIVING

As a dream image, giving provides clues about the nature of our relationships with others. For example, receiving many gifts on festive occasions such as a birthday emphasizes the esteem in which the dreamer is held by others, but if the gifts arrive at less appropriate times they can indicate the bombardment of unwelcome advice.

GIFTS THAT GO WRONG
A dream image that appears attractive on the outside, but is rotten or repulsive within, suggests disappointed expectations.

Buying a present can suggest our wish to make a special effort for the person concerned. On the other hand, showering presents on others, particularly if they are rejected, may indicate that the dreamer is being too thrusting in the gift of advice, lavishing attention where it is not wanted, or making inappropriate attempts to become acceptable to others.

Giving and Receiving

INCONGRUOUS GIFTS
A gift that appears inappropriate may indicate the unwelcome attentions of another person, or attributions, qualities or virtues in the dreamer of which he or she feels unworthy.

LETTERS AND PACKAGES

Letters and Packages

Receiving goods or messages through the mail often heralds something unexpected in the dreamer's life, such as a new opportunity or challenge.

The dreamer's response to the contents of the package may give clues to the meaning. For example, failure to take a letter out of the envelope may suggest that full use will not be made of the chance on offer, while a sense of anticipation before opening it can indicate a more positive attitude. The identity of the sender may also be important to the dream's meaning.

MESSAGES
BY MAIL
If the dreamer is acting as mailman, or is carrying a message for someone else, this may indicate a potential for responsibility, or for being trusted with secrets.

SHOPPING AND MONEY

Stores and shops often symbolize the array of opportunities and rewards that we encounter in our lives. Our ability to seize them may be signified by the amount of money we dream we have. Money generally represents power in Level 1 and 2 dreams (see page 42), and to find that one has

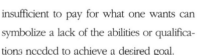

insufficient to pay for what one wants can symbolize a lack of the abilities or qualifications needed to achieve a desired goal.

STORE WINDOWS	HOARDING MONEY
These may suggest exclusion from the good things of life.	Hoarding can indicate both prudence and selfishness.

COMMUNICATION

PUBLIC SPEAKING
An audience that refuses to be quiet may relate to a general confusion of ideas. The absence of an audience suggests a total neglect of the dreamer's ideas by others, or a complete lack of recognition of his or her achievements.

Dreams often stress social vulnerabilities, and these may relate to the dreamer's inability to communicate effectively with others. Generally, such dreams portray the dreamer as unable to make himself or herself heard, or as desperately trying to attract attention, or to alert others to what the dreamer sees as an impending disaster of some kind. But we may also find ourselves being laughed at, or hearing others making disparaging remarks at our expense. Others may turn away in contempt when we try to give opinions or advice, or to embark upon conversation.

RULES AND REGULATIONS

Rules carry associations of structure, compulsion, control. If, in a dream, we seem to be giving strict instructions to others or to ourselves, then the dream may be drawing attention to a desire to make life more predictable. If it is others who are making the rules, the underlying message may be the need for more discipline in life.

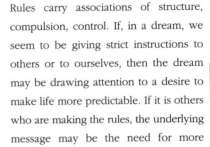

Dreams in which we stand accused of breaking rules of whose existence we were unaware emphasize the unfairness of many life experiences – such dreams may help

MISBEHAVIOUR Dreams in which the rebellious dreamer deliberately breaks rules often hark back to early childhood.

to release the dreamer's frustration.

Obeying rules can indicate that the dreamer is too easily led by others, but may also signify a sense of integrity.

Rules and Regulations

AT HOME

Domestic events are among the most common subject-matter for dreaming. Often the dream is set in the dreamer's own home, yet some of the details are strangely inaccurate. Items of furniture may be in the wrong place, domestic appliances may have changed in size, and total strangers may suddenly appear and treat the house as if it belongs to them.

Anomalies of this kind are sometimes used by the dream to draw attention to particular wishes or anxieties, to unlock hidden memories, or to prompt a fresh approach to some kind of problem. By using them as stimuli for direct or free association (see pages 58 and 228), the dreamer can often tease out the meaning of the dream, linking the everyday details to wider mythic, symbolic or archetypal themes.

COOKING

When food is being prepared for other people in a dream, this may indicate the dreamer's wish to influence others, or to make them dependent.

CRACKED OBJECTS

These suggest flaws in the dreamer's character, or in certain of his or her arguments, ideas or relationships.

OCCUPATIONS

Occupations feature prominently in dreams and usually relate to aspects of the dreamer's own personality. We may find ourselves trying in vain to sell newspapers, for example, which may signify an inability to alert others to important information of some kind. A dream of applying for a number of jobs could indicate that the dreamer needs to adopt a clearer sense of direction in life.

Often we may find ourselves dreaming of a current role or project, in which case the dream may be pointing out areas where we are functioning unproductively, misusing abilities or letting new opportunities slip by.

BUREAUCRACY
A dream of dealing with bureaucracy often relates to a lack of emotion, either in the dreamer or in those with whom he or she comes into contact.

SAILOR
Sailors typically represent the adventurous side of the dreamer, and the desire to explore the inner self.

WAITER
If the dreamer receives (or gives) good service, this may emphasize the importance of interdependence. Bad or aloof service can suggest the need for more interpersonal warmth.

POLICE
Police may represent inhibition, and the censorship of natural impulses by the conscious mind. Being

chased by the police can indicate a guilty conscience.

HOUSES AND BUILDINGS

Houses in dreams usually represent the dreamer, and can symbolize his or her body or the various levels of the mind. Like bodies, houses have fronts and backs, windows that look out onto the world and doors through which food is brought. It was from a dream of a house that Jung formulated his theory of the collective unconscious (see page 57).

Other buildings can also represent the self. Courts of law may symbolize

Houses and Buildings

LIBRARIES
This represents ideas and the ready availability of knowledge.

PLACES OF WORSHIP
A church, cathedral, mosque or temple often

represents the spiritual side of the dreamer, peace, or higher wisdom.

the dreamer's powers of judgment, and museums stand for the past, while factories or mills often relate to the creative side of the dreamer's life, emphasizing either its productivity or its mechanical, stereotypical nature.

Houses and Buildings

WINDOWS
Freud saw windows as feminine sexual symbols; Jung linked them to the dreamer's ability to understand the outside world.

DOORS
A door opening outward may show a need to be more accessible to others. A door opening inward invites self-exploration.

CASTLES
A castle may remind us that our psychological defences may be isolating us from others.

UNFINISHED HOUSES
Work is required on some aspects of mind or body.

ROOMS AND FLOORS
Living rooms represent the conscious and pre-conscious, cellars the unconscious, and upper rooms the dreamer's spirituality.

OBJECTS

Objects

The dream world is littered with objects, some familiar to the dreamer, some unrecognizable. All have potential significance, and it can be the more obscure things that provide the richest associations and amplifications in dream interpretation.

SHELLS
The shell is a symbol that often represents the unconscious and the imagination.

**CLOCKS
AND WATCHES**
Clocks and watches stand for the human heart, and thus the dreamer's emotional life.

BOOKS
Books may represent wisdom. Inability to read a book indicates the need to develop greater powers of concentration.

GARBAGE CANS
A garbage can signifies unwanted memories or duties, or aspects of the self that the dreamer wishes to discard.

Objects

However, some associations clearly link to waking experience. A camera, for example, often represents a wish to preserve the past, while hiding things in obscure places may stand for a wish for self-concealment. Similarly, a statue or bust often represents the desire to place someone or something on a pedestal,

MIRRORS
A strange face in the mirror often indicates an identity crisis. If the face is frightening, it may stand for the Shadow.

and may also signify their remoteness. A candle or torch suggests the intellect, or other, more spiritual forms of understanding, while a chest or casket can evoke various meanings, ranging from childhood to forbidden knowledge. The object's function is usually its most important aspect, although shape, colour and texture can also be significant.

AT SCHOOL

School experiences frequently appear in adults' dreams. Sometimes the dream relates to specific happenings that still fill the dreamer with remembered pride or (more often) embarrassment, but sometimes it uses a generic school as a convenient metaphor to convey its message. Dreams of finding oneself back at school, but demoted to a lower class, or stripped of some coveted responsibility, symbolize childhood insecurities that have still not been resolved.

A SCHOOL BAG A full school bag can relate to the dreamer's accumulated knowledge, and desire to continue learning. If the bag is heavy or uncomfortable, this may signify that the past is a burden.

THE CLASSROOM

The dream classroom can represent learning, nostalgia, competition, or the need to re-think aspects of one's personal, social or professional life.

The school teacher is a classic symbol for authority, and may represent the father or mother, an elder sibling, or the dreamer's love for or fear of those who have determined the course of his or her life. Alternatively, a teacher may stand for that censoring aspect of the dreamer's personality that keeps the more unruly impulses in check.

THEATRES AND THE CIRCUS

All the dream world is a stage, a theatre in which magical transformations take place. Some dreams use theatres, cinemas or circuses as their setting. Such dreams are usually imbued with a particular clarity and vividness.

A dream theatre may appear to offer the dreamer an understanding of the mystery that lies behind the world of appearances. However, the dreamer may also find the theatre or circus ring empty, or the cinema screen blank, and experience a haunting loneliness, as if he or she is excluded from the revelation that is about to appear to others.

If we actually find ourselves on the stage, or in the circus ring, participating in the drama, we may identify with the character or behaviour on display. But if the dreamer is merely an onlooker, this can indicate a danger of being taken in by the powers of illusion or an unfulfilled wish to throw off the conventions of ordinary existence.

Theatres and the Circus

ACROBAT

The acrobat represents the combination of strength and grace, and thus the union of male and female. Trapeze artists may signify spiritual courage.

RING-MASTER

The ring-master commands the skills of humans and animals, yet performs no acts himself. He feeds upon others, and his presence in a dream may indicate the ultimately barren nature of this kind of power.

CLOWN

The clown is an aspect of the archetypal Trickster (see pages 70–71), making a fool of himself or herself in order to mock the pretentiousness and absurd posturing of others.

TOWNS AND CITIES

Just as the house stands for the self in Jungian psychology, so the town or city represents the social environment beyond the self, including family and friends, and the whole network of responsibilities which enfolds us.

A busy town, or one with doors and windows open, may represent the warmth of the dreamer's relationships with others; while a town with wide, empty streets or vast, desolate piazzas can indicate a sense of isolation or rejection from society.

WALLED CITY
The dream may be suggesting that exclusion is necessary if the dreamer's social values are to be maintained, or it may be questioning the usefulness of a "wall" that already exists.

A large, impersonal city may suggest that the dreamer has many acquaintances but few close friends, and the dream may be indicating the need to establish more intimate relationships. If the houses are vague and shadowy, this may indicate the dreamer's lack of understanding of other people, or lack of self-knowledge. A city beneath the ground or the sea often relates to the dreamer's unconscious.

HILL TOWN
A town or city on a hill often suggests wisdom, heaven, the home of the gods, or the stronghold of the righteous.

HARBOUR
A harbour may represent people whom the dreamer has to leave behind.

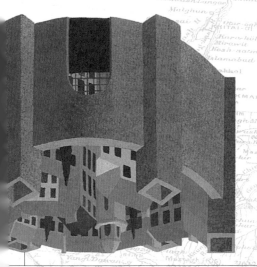

RUINED CITY
A ruined city may be drawing the dreamer's attention to a neglect of social relationships, or of aims or ideals in life.

The Elements and Seasons

THE ELEMENTS AND SEASONS

The elements and the seasons are often associated with Level 3 dreams (see page 42), because they relate to the natural energies and rhythms of life and thus serve as powerful symbols both of the dreamer's own being and of significant life changes.

Rivers and streams are strong metaphors for the passing of time. Water is a potent symbol of the unconscious, and attempts to dam a river may indicate that the dreamer is trying to repress material that is flowing from the unconscious mind.

RAINBOWS
Universally auspicious symbols, rainbows stand for redemption, good news, promise and forgiveness.

SNOW
Dreams often use snow to symbolize transformation and purification.

LIGHTNING
This suggests inspiration, but warns that flashes of brilliance can be destructive.

THE SEA
Jung believed that turning to face the sea indicates that the dreamer is prepared to confront the unconscious.

Spring is an obvious signal of new beginnings, while high summer indicates achievement and the need to savour life's pleasures. Summer also symbolizes the conscious mind, far-sightedness and clarity of thought. Autumn and winter represent the unconscious and the darker, hidden side of the dreamer's self, but may also indicate that a fallow period is called for, a time of incubation before new ideas burst forth. Autumn and winter can also denote that even in the midst of apparent death, life goes on, working its mysteries unseen until the time for regeneration and re-birth.

WATER AND AIR
Air is associated with wisdom lightly worn, and clarity of thought. Air is the element that symbolizes otherworldly concerns. Water symbolizes the unconscious, the depths of the imagination, the source of creativity.

The Elements and Seasons

FIRE AND EARTH
Fire is a masculine energy, and represents that which is overt, positive and conscious. The earth can symbolize fertility and, like water, can represent the feminine.

ALCHEMY
At the centre of this diagram is the "fifth essence", which has appeared in some dreams.

ANIMALS

Animals are particularly powerful dream symbols, and usually carry a universal meaning, although they can also appear as specific animals known to the dreamer, in which case their significance tends to be personal. As well as real animals, dreams may also make use of animals encountered in films, myths or fairytales. Sometimes, too, there may be a reference to animal associations embedded in the similes and clichés of idiomatic language (linking foxes with cunning, elephants with long memories, pigs with gluttony, and so on).

BUTTERFLIES
Butterflies have often been used to symbolize the soul and its transformation after death.

Animals have always signified our natural, instinctive and sometimes baser energies and desires, and in dreams they often draw our attention to undervalued or repressed aspects of the self. Devouring an animal can represent the assimilation of natural wisdom.

Animals in dreams may be frightening or friendly, wild or tame, and their

Animals

demeanour can be an important clue for interpretation. They may even speak or change their form.

BIRDS
In most cultures, birds symbolize the higher self. The dove frequently stands for peace.

FISH
Fish often symbolize divinity. They can also represent insights into the unconscious.

MONKEYS
Monkeys in dreams often represent the playful, mischievous side of the dreamer.

HORSE
In dreams the horse generally symbolizes humankind's harnessing of the forces of nature.

LION
The lion almost invariably appears in dreams as a regal symbol of power and pride.

WILD BEASTS
Freud saw wild animals as representing passionate impulses of which the dreamer is ashamed.

NUMBERS AND SHAPES

ONE
The prime mover from which all manifest creation flows, the source of all life.

TWO
The number of duality, divine symmetry and the union of male and female.

THREE
The number of synthesis and of the union of body, mind and spirit.

FOUR
The number of the square, harmony, and the stability on which the world depends.

FIVE
The number of the five-pointed star that represents humankind.

Popular dream interpretation has always placed great significance upon the occurrence of numbers and shapes.

Jung noticed that as his clients progressed toward psychological health, mandala-like shapes and designs, with squares and circles radiating from a central point, began to feature with increasing prominence in their dreams. Once Jung had identified this geometrical archetype, he found its equivalents in all the myths and belief systems of the world.

Numbers, which can also represent archetypal energies of the collective unconscious, may not be given directly in dreams. In dream recall, the dreamer may be aware that objects or characters were presented in certain numerical patterns, or that actions tended to be carried out a set number of times. Dream interpretation and amplification can focus upon these numbers and identify the significance that they carry for the dreamer.

Numbers and Shapes

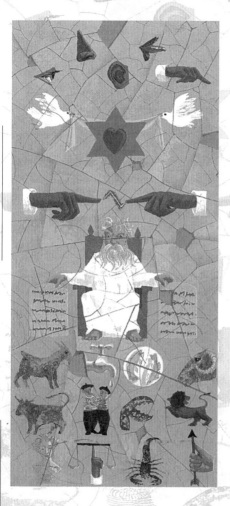

SIX
The number of love, in dreams six stands for a movement toward inner harmony.

SEVEN
Seven symbolizes risk and opportunity, and the power of inner transformation.

EIGHT
This is the symbol of regeneration and new beginnings.

NINE
The number of indestructibility and eternity, of three multiplied by itself.

TEN
This is the number that represents both the law and the ten commandments.

Numbers and Shapes

COLOURS

Colours

BROWN
Brown usually represents the earth. For Freud it was a symbol of anal fixation.

RED
Red is widely known as the colour of vitality, passion, anger and sexual arousal.

ORANGE
The colour of fertility, hope, new beginnings, and the dawning of spirituality.

Colours are often one of the most revealing aspects of dream imagery. The meaning of dream colours varies from one individual to another, depending upon the associations held in the unconscious, although universal meanings also come into play. The primary colours are usually most significant. Violet, a combination of red and blue, has an especially mystical quality, suggesting both a union and a tension between the dual creative forces behind the universe. Traditionally, gold and silver stand for sun and moon, masculine and feminine, day and night. For Jung, these hues represented the conscious and unconscious minds.

YELLOW
Yellow can represent the wise use of authority.

GREEN
Colour of nature, the elements and regeneration.

BLUE
Blue is usually a highly spiritual dream colour.

SOUNDS AND VOICES

Dream sounds should not be neglected during interpretation. Music especially tends to be laden with meaning. It may be that a melody has personal associations, or it could be the title or the lyrics that are significant. Alternatively, music may carry a message of its own, even when the melody is unrecognized or not remembered upon waking. Strange, half-heard voices can have the same mystic quality, often suggesting that the dreamer should listen to the promptings of inner wisdom.

BUGLES
A call to action, suggesting that the dreamer must arouse his or her hidden potential.

Sounds and Voices

WHISTLING
This can carry magical overtones, as in whistling for a wind.

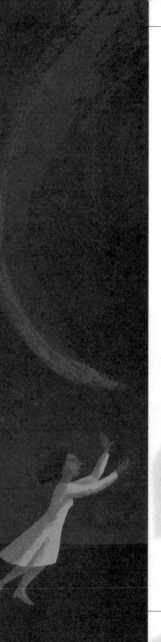

GHOSTS AND DEMONS

The witches, vampires, were-wolves and half-seen ghosts of children's dreams often symbolize those aspects of the self that the child is unable to understand or integrate into his or her worldview. If childhood monsters persist into the dreams of adulthood, it could be that the work of comprehension and integration remains uncompleted. The dreamer may be still trying to reduce reality to safe and predictable dimensions.

As with all nightmares, such dreams serve the purpose of urging the dreamer to turn and face the pursuing dark forces, and to see that it is only fear that turns them into monsters. By recognizing and accepting the many energies that make up our psyche, we may in time come to a better understanding of our conscious and unconscious minds, where most of the mysteries of life reside.

Ghosts and Demons

GHOSTS

The image of a ghost as a shadowy being may suggest hidden knowledge within the dreamer or fear of death or of an afterlife bereft of sensation.

GIANTS

The monster or giant who towers over a small and vulnerable child is an archetypal theme in children's dreams and stories. Such figures often represent dominating adults in the child's life. By confronting these monsters in their dreams, children can come to terms with them in their emotional lives.

IMPOSSIBILITIES

ABSURDITIES
Dreams often juxtapose seemingly incompatible elements. These remind the dreamer of life's infinite possibilities – be more adventurous.

Impossibilities

Dreams remind us that our normal way of perceiving reality is only one of many possible states of consciousness. Dreams may deliberately distort waking reality, producing new juxtapositions of ideas and experiences, which give rise to new patterns of thought or behaviour.

When a dream presents material that appears impossible to the waking mind, this incongruity may be the crux of the meaning. One manifestation of this is the reversed relationship. A platform, for

example, may move toward a train, perhaps emphasizing to the dreamer the need to approach life from a completely new perspective. The dreamer may appear in the opposite sex, drawing attention to his or her neglect of the Anima or Animus, the female aspect of man and the male aspect of woman. Such reversals may be aiming to teach the dreamer that seeing everything in terms of opposites is limiting: only by uniting our various energies can we realize our full potential.

TALKING PAINTINGS
Dreams in which the characters in a picture talk or come to life may emphasize ways in which fantasies help or hinder the dreamer's psychological development.

TRANSFORMATIONS

Transformations play a major role in our dreams. Often they serve to link dream images together in the way that a dissolve does in a film. Equally, they can be meaningful in their own right, drawing attention to relationships between different aspects of our lives, and between the various preoccupations of the unconscious.

Sometimes a whole scene will transform itself into another, like a vision conjured by an enchanter. It is relatively commonplace too for the dreamer himself or herself to change – for example, from man to woman, from young to old, from victor to victim.

In the process of dream analysis, transformations can sometimes provide

BECOMING A PLANT

This is normally an image of nurture and integration.

the most important clues. An untidy or dirty room that suddenly becomes clean and bright can signify the end of moral or spiritual danger; an animal transformed into a human being can represent a redirection or transcendence of the dreamer's primal instincts; a human transformed into an animal can stand for a descent to the more fundamental levels of the psyche, or for the rediscovery of more natural, spontaneous emotions.

Agents of transformation, such as the wizard, the magician or the shaman, may appear as dream characters. They stand outside the rational, social world, but have the power to change it.

Transformations

TRANSFORMED HOUSE
A house transformed into something else is likely to be a comment by the dream on the state of the dreamer's psyche.

WORDS INTO IMAGES
Puns based on dream images may enable the dreaming mind to give visual form to abstract qualities.

MYTH AND LEGEND

If dreams and myths stem from the same roots in the collective unconscious, as Jung believed, then it is not surprising that mythical elements are often found in dreams.

Jung recommended the use of myths as a repertoire of parallels which would help a dreamer tease out the meaning of a dream – the process of amplification (see page 58). With Level 3 dreams (see page 42), amplification is made easier by the fact that the dream material often contains explicit mythological themes: these represent the archetypal energies of the collective unconscious in personalized form, and indicate the

MERMAID
The mermaid embodies the Anima – a temptress who lures the overt, active, male energies of the conscious mind into the depths of the unconscious.

THE HERO
The Hero may represent the noble side of the unconscious mind – the part not bound by conventional wisdom.

relationship of such energies to the particular life-circumstances of the dreamer.

Mythic images occurring in the dreams of Westerners often call to mind Greek, Egyptian and Christian equivalents – the mythologies with which many of us are most familiar. The Resurrected God, the Hero, the Saviour, the Trickster, the Wise Old Man and the Young Girl are all recurring archetypes. Sometimes the mythic content is undisguised: a princess

in a tower, for example. However, there are also oblique references, such as a Hero expressed as a star from sport or the movies, or as someone coming valiantly to the rescue in a recognizably modern context.

Myth and Legend

DIONYSOS
In dreams, the Greek god of wine, nature, fertility and divine ecstasy can stand for heightened states of consciousness or a recognition of our instinctive primal energies.

STARS AND PLANETS

Level 3 dreams about the heavens often convey a sense of the eternal, unchanging nature of ultimate reality. Rarely, even in Level 1 and Level 2 dreams, do the stars and planets carry negative connotations, although some dreamers interpret them as emphasizing the insignificance of human life in the face of the vast impersonal forces of the universe.

Occasionally, the dreaming mind will use planets to convey metaphorical meaning, drawing upon their links with mythology. Mars is associated with war, passion and rage, Venus with love and eroticism, Jupiter with fullness, pleasure and well-being, Saturn with wisdom, masculinity and (sometimes) Pan or the Devil.

Planets normally appear singly in dreams, but if there is more than one, it may be their juxtaposition that is important. The sun and

STARS

As well as representing fate and the celestial powers, the stars can stand for the dreamer's higher states of consciousness. A single star shining more brightly than the rest can signify success in competition with others, but may also serve to remind the dreamer of his or her responsibilities to those of lesser ability.

moon together may represent the relationship between the conscious and unconscious, rational and irrational, while Saturn and Venus can stand for the relationship between male and female.

THE MOON
The moon often represents the feminine aspect, the queen of the night, and the mystery of hidden, secret things.

THE SUN
The sun has connotations of the masculine, the world of overt things, the conscious mind, the intellect, and the father.

COMETS
Dreamers often associate comets with a warning of dazzling, temporary success, followed by rapid descent and eventual destruction. Comets also represent inspiration.

WORKING WITH DREAMS

The first stage of working with dreams is the art of recalling them; many people claim never to, and some deny having dreams. However, with practice you may remember each morning.

Remembering dreams is a habit, and can be cultivated. The best way is to tell yourself during the day that you will remember your dreams, and upon awakening, focus your conscious mind for a while on whatever ideas or emotions have emerged from your sleep, and allow them to prompt dream recall.

Keeping a dream diary makes it possible to build up a detailed picture of your dream life. Write down (or sketch) literally everything you can remember and make a note of any emotions or associations that emerge. Be patient: it may take weeks or months before you regularly remember your dreams,

but persevere. The process can be speeded up by setting an alarm clock for two hours or so after you usually fall asleep: you will stand a good chance of awakening immediately after the first, dream-laden period of REM Rapid Eye Movement) sleep.

Some dream researchers advise subjects to collect at least 100 dreams, which should allow enough time for the common themes to emerge coherently. It is always worth searching for connections with the events of the day, but remember – the dream has a reason for choosing these events, and may be using them to symbolize deeper material. If events are sparking off any memories, these may lead back to long-forgotten experiences.

Keeping a Dream Record

A dream sketchbook can really capture a dream. Making notes immediately after waking requires a mental adjustment that will often interpose itself between the

"I saw a hairy caterpillar which changed into the keyboard of a typewriter. The paper coming out of the machine had glistening rain-drops on it – but there was no rain. The caterpillar turned into a butterfly and flew off. Suddenly, I was in a rain storm trying to bring in laundry."

Rain is linked with purification. The caterpillar and butterfly symbol-ize awakening.

Keeping a Dream Record

dreamer and the dream, whereas a sketch can be made without losing touch with the dream. The example here is a dream by a 15-year-old girl: her spoken account is given on page 223, with a note on the symbolism above; the sketch from her visual note-book is reproduced opposite.

DREAM ANALYSIS

The best way to analyze dreams is through the recurring themes that emerge from a dream diary. A good way to start is to separate the dream material into discrete categories: for example, scenery, objects, characters, events, colours, emotions. Try not to ignore apparently unimportant details – these may carry the most meaning.

Start by selecting something from one of the categories, and subject it to the process of Jungian direct association (see page 58). Write down the object (or whatever) in the centre of a piece of paper and note down all the associated images and ideas that come to you. Try to ensure that each association is specific: if the dream contained a red car, it may be its colour, rather than the fact that it is a car, that is of most symbolic significance. Do the same for each dream symbol until all the categories have been covered.

Dream Analysis

Dream Analysis

If few associations arise, the dream may be operating at Level 1 (see page 42), simply serving as a reminder of the significance of certain events in the dreamer's life. It may be hinting, for example, that particular emotions be acknowledged.

If the dream appears to carry a further level of meaning, Freudian free association may be helpful, allowing the mind freely to follow a chain of thoughts and images set off by the individual dream element. This method can reveal repressed memories, urges or emotions.

If the memories and ideas that emerge from dreams are purely personal associations, they probably emerge from a Level 2 dream, but if they seem to be working as archetypal symbols (see pages 65–77) they are probably at Level 3. For these "grand dreams" Jung recommended, as a further way of teasing out their meaning, amplification (see page 58), a technique to establish parallels between dream symbols and the archetypal imagery stored in the collective unconscious.

DREAM CONTROL

The ability regularly to become more conscious in our dreams is known as lucid dreaming (see pages 31–44), and is often found in people who have a high degree of concentration and awareness in waking life. There are several techniques for establishing awareness in dreams, and thus for experiencing them with the conscious mind.

The reflection technique involves asking oneself as often as possible during the day, "How do I know that I am not

Dream Control

dreaming now?", and being as specific as possible with the answers. It then becomes easier to recognize an actual dream for what it is, and so assert control over it. A variation on this is the intention technique, in which the dreamer constantly tells himself or herself during the day that particular events in the dream world will be recognized as such by the aware, dreaming mind. If, for example, we frequently dream of horses, or trains, or schools, we should impress upon our waking mind that the appearance of such objects in dreams will alert us to the fact of dreaming.

A similar technique is to imagine ourselves dreaming of certain common objects or actions, like climbing stairs, and attempt to visualize them as frequently as possible in waking life. Again, when the chosen image occurs in a dream, we become conscious of dreaming.

Autosuggestion, repeating to oneself again and again on the verge of our sleep that conscious awareness will

Dream Control

emerge in our dreams, can also help.

An approach used by various Eastern traditions and by Jung in his technique of active imagination, is to imagine that one is dreaming while awake. Thus we enter a "virtual" waking dream world: everything is seen as an illusion which has been created by the mind, and can be changed at will. By reminding ourselves constantly that we are exercising this will when carrying out every waking action, we can potentially build a bridge between waking and dream consciousness, thus creating a single level of awareness that extends throughout waking, dreaming and dreamless sleep.

A similar technique of mind control is to develop the habit of asking ourselves when remembering dreams why an unusual dream event did not prompt us into realizing that we were dreaming. This technique trains the mind by reminding it of its past failures to alert us to the fact of dreaming, and encourages it not to repeat such failures.

Many of the above techniques can be used in conjunction with each other as aids to lucid dreaming, as can more conventional methods, such as keeping a dream diary or meditation. However, a key requirement for all dream-control techniques is patience – do not be too discouraged if the desired results are some time in coming.

It is also vital not to try too hard. Lucid dreaming is achieved by an act of will, but not by an act of teeth-gritting determination. Like any creative activity, it is most readily achieved by a mind that is concentrated, motivated and persistent, but at the same time light and playful.

SOLVING PROBLEMS

The prescription that we should sleep on problems is well known. Although the conscious ego is inactive while we sleep, some part of the mind continues working on the problems that beset it during the day, so that when we awake the solutions may already be in place.

Sometimes answers are actually given in dreams. A famous example is that of the German chemist Friedrich Kekulé who claimed that his discovery of the molecular structure of benzene, in 1961, came to him in a dream.

We can sometimes obtain a demonstration of the problem-solving power of the dreaming mind if we visualize an unsolved anagram or mathematical puzzle while drifting to sleep. Instructing the mind to work on the puzzle can often stimulate a dream solution.

The answer may come literally, unfiltered by symbols. The Russian chemist

Solving Problems

Dmitri Mendeleev, after many fruitless attempts to tabulate the elements according to their atomic weight, dreamed their respective values and subsequently found all but one to be correct, a discovery that led to the publication of his periodic law in 1869.

When dreams offer symbolic rather than literal solutions, interpretation can be more difficult. The scientist Neils Bohr identified the model of a hydrogen atom in 1913 after a dream in which he stood on the sun and saw the planets attached to its surface by thin filaments as they circled overhead. Numerical solutions, in particular, may be conveyed in symbolic form, perhaps using associations that are lodged deep in the personal unconscious.

NIGHTMARES
Psychological problems can also be solved through dreams. Anxiety dreams can help us recognize important truths about ourselves. The original meaning of "nightmare" comes from an evil spirit that visited people in their sleep to seduce and so gain possession of them. The "mare", or demon, came to women as an incubus (shown in the 18th-century painting by Henry Fuseli, above) and to men as a succubus, leaving the dreamer feeling oppressed.

SELECT BIBLIOGRAPHY

Boss, M. *"I Dreamt Last Night": A New Approach to the Revelations of Dreaming and its Uses in Psychotherapy*. New York: Gardener, 1977.

Dement, W. *"Effect of sleep deprivation"*. Science 131, 1705–1707, 1960.

Faraday, A. *Dream Power: The Use of Dreams in Everyday Life*. London: Pan Books, 1972.

Garfield, P. *Creative Dreaming*. London: Futura, 1976.

Garfield P. *The Healing Power of Dreams*. New York and London: Simon & Schuster, 1991

Hall, C. S., and Nordby, V. J. *The Individual and His Dreams*. New York: New American Library, 1972

Hillman, J. *The Essential James Hillman*. London: Routledge, 1989.

Jung, C.G. *Analytical Psychology: Its Theory and Practice*. London and New York: Ark 1986.

Jung, C.G. *Dream Analysis*. London and New York: Routledge, 1984.

Jung, C.G. *Dreams*. Princeton, NJ: Princeton University Press, 1974.

Jung, C.G. *Four Archetypes*. London and New York: Routledge, 1972.

Jung, C.G. *Memories, Dreams, Reflections*. London: Fontana, 1967.

Jung, C.G. *Psychology and Alchemy*. London and New York: Routledge, 1980.

Jung, C.G. *Selected Writings*. London: Fontana (Harper Collins), 1983.

Jung, C.G. *Two Essays on Analytical Psychology*. Second edition. London: Routledge, 1992.

Kleitman, N. *Sleep and Wakefulness*. 2nd edition. Chicago: University of Chicago Press, 1963.

Mattoon, M.A. *Applied Dream Analysis: a Jungian Approach*. London: John Wiley & Sons, 1978.

Mavromatis, A. *Hypnogogia*. London and New York: Routledge, 1987.

Snyder, F. *"The new biology of dreaming"*. Arch. Gen. Psychiat. 8, pp 381-391, 1963.

Tholey, P. "Techniques for inducing and manipulating lucid dreams". *Perceptual and Motor Skills*, 57, pp 79–90, 1983.

Ullman, M., Krippner, S., and Vaughan, A. *Dream Telepathy: Experiments in Nocturnal ESP*. 2nd edition. Jefferson NC: McFarland, 1989.

Ullman, M., and Limmer, C. (eds.) *The Variety of Dream Experience*. London: Crucible, 1989.

Ullman, M., and Zimmerman, N. *Working With Dreams*. New York: Eleanor Friede Books, 1987.

Van de Castle, R. *The Psychology of Dreaming*. Morristown, N.J: General Learning Press, 1971.

Whitmont, E. C., and Perera, S. B. *Dreams, a Portal to the Source*. London: Routledge, 1989.

NOTES ON THE TEXT

DREAMS AND SLEEP

p23 REM sleep was discovered by Nathaniel Kleitman and Eugene Aserinsky at the University of Chicago in 1953. Research in the early 1960s revealing four distinct levels of sleep was led by the physiologist Frederick Snyder. As early as the 1930s, it was noted that eye movement while sleeping is strongly linked with dreaming.

LUCID DREAMS

p31 Research by Jayne Gackenbach (b.1946) showed that lucid dreamers appear to suffer less from depression and neuroses.

PRECOGNITION AND ESP

p35 Prof. Hans Bender, of the University of Freiburg, Germany, collected a large number of verifiable precognitive dream accounts. Many dreams foretelling the sinking of the *Titanic* were collected by Prof. Ian Stevenson of the University of Virginia.

LEVELS OF MEANING

p41 The Jungian analyst Mary Mattoon believes that proof for the existence of the collective unconscious can also be found in other areas of psychology, linguistics and anthropology.

THE NATURE OF DREAMING

p46 The British psychologist Anne Faraday and Ian Oswald from the University of Edinburgh led the 1970s research into dream recall and amnesia.

FREUD ON DREAMS

p48 Ernest Jones (1879–1958) is the most extensive and reliable writer on Freud's theories about dreams. He developed Freud's ideas and between 1953 and 1957 wrote the three-volume biography of Freud for which he is best known.

CHANGE AND TRANSITION

p115 It was the American psychologists Thomas Holmes and Richard Rahe who discovered that individuals are prone to physical illness for up to two years after major changes in life-circumstances.

SOLVING PROBLEMS

p234 In *On the Nightmare* (1910), Ernest Jones drew a parallel between the medieval belief in "mares" and Freudian dream theory. He found the incubus to be an apt dream metaphor for medieval men's horror of homosexuality and women's fear of their own sexual urges.

DREAM INDEX

Dream Index

Dream Index

SUBJECT INDEX

ACKNOWLEDGMENTS

The publishers wish to thank the following individuals, museums, and photographic libraries for permission to reproduce their material. Every care has been taken to trace copyright holders; however, if we have omitted anyone we apologize and will, if informed, make corrections in any future edition.

Page 37 Popperfoto, Northampton; **48** W.E. Freud Collection, London/Mary Evans Picture Library, London; **56** Mary Evans Picture Library, London; **140–141** Zefa, London; **155** Mary Evans Picture Library, London; **201** Popperfoto, Northampton; **204** Newman/NHPA, Ardingly; **217** Musee des Augustins, Toulouse/Bridgeman Art Library, London; **218–219** Nasa/Science Photo Library, London; **223** NHPA, Ardingly; **224** NHPA, Ardingly; **235** Detroit Institute of Art, Michigan/Bridgeman Art Library, London.

COMMISSIONED ARTWORK CREDITS
Hugh Dixon: 80–81, 123, 130, 133, 140, 143, 145, 160–161, 180–181, 182, 212

Ricca Kawai: 224

Peter Malone: 1, 2, 10, 12, 14–15, 24, 32, 40, 42, 45, 47, 63, 88, 90, 92–93, 112, 113, 114, 115, 116, 117, 120–121, 126–127, 128, 130–131, 147, 149, 153, 156–157, 162–163, 164–165, 166, 167, 169, 171, 172, 176–177, 178, 179, 181, 183, 185, 188, 192–193, 195, 197, 198–199, 200–201, 202, 204–205, 207, 208, 210, 212, 213, 215, 216–217, 220, 222, 227, 235

Paul Redgrave: 72–73

Jim Robbins: 84-5, 122-3, 131, 135, 150-1, 152-3, 164-5, 166, 168-9, 170-1, 176, 181, 182, 183, 193, 213

COMMISSIONED PHOTOGRAPHY AND PHOTOGRAPHIC ILLUSTRATION CREDITS:
Jules Selmes: 35, 43, 44, 46, 49, 61, 78, 80–81, 84, 100, 104, 106–107, 108, 110–111, 116, 119, 122, 127, 129, 130, 132, 133, 135, 136–139, 141, 142, 143, 144, 145, 149, 150, 152, 154, 156, 156–157, 158, 159, 160, 161, 162–163, 164, 166, 168, 170, 172, 173, 174, 175, 176, 177, 178, 179, 180, 181, 182, 184, 186, 187, 189, 190, 191, 193, 194, 195, 196, 197, 198–199, 200–201, 204, 205, 209, 210, 211, 214, 215, 223, 229, 231, 235